A. L. A. RULES FOR
Filing Catalog Cards

A. L. A. RULES FOR
Filing Catalog Cards

Prepared by a Special Committee
SOPHIE K. HISS, CHAIRMAN

AMERICAN LIBRARY ASSOCIATION
CHICAGO, ILLINOIS, 1942

PUBLISHER'S NOTE

The rules presented in this volume are offered as representing the best accepted practice. The presentation of the material, particularly the showing of relationships, has presented many problems. Users are urged to send comment, criticisms and suggestions to the publishers to the end that reprints or revised editions may better serve their purpose.

Preface

THE arrangement of cards in the dictionary catalogs of American libraries has been influenced to a large extent by the principles laid down by C. A. Cutter in his *Rules for a printed dictionary catalogue* in 1876 and revised in a final (4th) edition in 1904. The many variations to be found in present-day library practice have grown out of differences in the interpretation and in the expansion of the Cutter rules; and also, in part, out of a need felt in many libraries for a simplification of the Cutter classed arrangements.

The present code is based on a comparative study of filing rules which have appeared in printed codes and in manuals of library science; and also of the practices in a number of large and medium-sized public and university libraries. The comparison showed few rules with no variants; some rules where a generally accepted practice is clearly indicated; many rules where two practices are in equal use and apparently equally satisfactory; and finally, in regard to the more perplexing problems of arrangement, a wide diversity of practice and opinion.

The code attempts to provide a set of alphabeting rules in accord with the most generally accepted usage. In addition, it offers rules for both a grouped and an alphabetic order of arrangement under certain types of headings. The grouped arrangement is suitable when a large number of entries is to be filed under an author, a place or a subject heading, but it depends for clearness and ease in consultation upon a very full and carefully planned system of guide-cards and upon explicit directions to the users of the catalog. The alphabetic arrangement is self-explanatory and is probably easier to consult when entries under place or subject are being sought. In the absence of a definite knowledge as to the psychological approach of the user to the catalog, it does not seem advisable to insist dogmatically that one alternative is to be preferred to the other. The size of the catalog, the character of the collection, and the nature of the clientele to be served will influence the choice of alternative. Consistency throughout the catalog is in general desirable but may be disregarded in special instances provided that the guide-cards at the given point show with precision the order adopted.

The separation of the subject catalog from the author and title catalog, which in recent years has been adopted by a number of libraries, does not require changes in the general alphabeting rules. The divided catalog simplifies to some extent the problem of the order of entries, but does not alter the arrangement within each type entry.

The code does not attempt to distinguish between, or to suggest, cataloging practices, except insofar as to call attention to an occasional detail that makes clearer the filing of an entry. The cataloger should keep constantly in mind the filer's problems and exercise care in cataloging details that may render filing and finding easier. In order to avoid confusion, since cataloging practices are not uniform, the examples in the following rules have been selected from entries that conform to the American Library Association or the Library of Congress cataloging rules.

For the convenience of small libraries, a selected list of recommended rules, together with a comprehensive example, will be found in Appendix V.

A.L.A. FILING CODE SUBCOMMITTEE
Mary Burnham
James B. Childs
Emily Hollowell
Ruth N. Latshaw
Amy C. Moon
Linda H. Morley
Nouvart Tashjian
Elizabeth E. Wilson
Sophie K. Hiss, *Chairman*

Contents

APPENDIXES

Explanatory Note

In this work subject entries are indicated by full capitalization throughout.

A.L.A. Rules for Filing Catalog Cards

1. Basic rule

  a) Arrange all entries according to the order of the English alphabet. *See also* Modified letters (Rule 2): Signs and symbols (Rule 3)

  b) Arrange word by word, alphabeting letter by letter to the end of each word.

New Amsterdam	not	New Amsterdam
New England		Newark
New wives for old		New England
Newark		Newman
Newman		New wives for old

2. Modified letters (umlaut, special letters)

  a) Disregard the modification of all letters, including the umlaut. Arrange ä, á, å, ē, ī, ö, ó, ő, ø, ü, ű, as a, e, i, o, u; ç, ć, č, ł, ñ, š, ž, as c, l, n, s, z.

> There are a number of other modifications which in transliteration from Oriental and other languages show dots or lines above or below the letters.[1] These will cause no difficulty in a general catalog if disregarded. Libraries requiring a different arrangement, as in a special language catalog, should adopt rules in accordance with the usage of the language.

In the case of headings with an umlaut in the first syllable, cross references should be made from, and to, the form spelled with an *e*.

Muel, Leon	Mullen, Allen
Muellenbach, Ernst	Müllen, Gustav
Mueller	Müllendorf
see also Muller (or Müller)	Muller (or Müller)
Mueller, Alfred Don	see also Muller
Muenscher, Joseph	Müller, Adam
La muerta de Néron	Muller, Adam L
Mullen (or Müllen)	Münchener bienen-zeitung
see also Muellen	

---

[1] For the alphabets and diacritical marks used in foreign languages, see U.S. Govt. print. off., *Manual of foreign languages for the use of printers and translators.* 3d ed. (Washington: Govt. print. off., 1936.)

This is the recommended treatment of the umlaut. It is the practice followed in many German reference books and is simpler for the majority of the users of the catalog who are unaware of the philological significance of the umlaut. For libraries that prefer to recognize the German umlaut and to treat in like manner similarly marked vowels in other languages, the following alternative rule is given.

  b) ALTERNATIVE RULE: File ä, ö, ü, in the Finnish, German, Hungarian, Scandinavian and modern Turkish languages as if written ae, oe, ue. This includes also the Hungarian ő and ű and the Danish-Norwegian ø.

File the Scandinavian å as aa.

```
Muel, Leon                Münchener bienen-zeitung
Muellen (or Müllen)       La muerta de Néron
   see also Mullen        Mullen
Müllen, Gustav               see also Muellen (or Müllen)
Muellenbach, Ernst        Mullen, Allen
Müllendorf                Muller
Mueller (or Müller)          see also Mueller (or Müller)
   see also Muller        Müller
Müller, Adam                 (This name is filed as if spelled
Mueller, Alfred Don          Mueller)
                          Muller, Adam L
```

  c) Arrange other special letters as follows: [2]
  (1) The Latin i and j as distinct letters.
  (2) The gothic type v (for u) and vv (for w) as u and w.
  (3) The Dutch ÿ (a manuscript form for ij) as ij.[3]
  (4) Typographical characters and abbreviations used in Latin incunabula as if written in full.[4]

3. Signs and symbols

  a) Signs without letters (used as author heading)

Arrange signs without preceding letters, when used instead of the author's name, before the letter A. Disregard the signs and subarrange by title; but if the signs are followed by titles of honor or forenames, subarrange by them. Signs alone precede signs followed by titles of honor, etc.

Signs at the beginning of a title, such as . . . or - -, are also to be disregarded, the title being arranged by the word following the signs.

---

[2] Transliteration rules for the non-Roman alphabets are printed in the revised *A.L.A. Catalog Rules.* Card rules for the transliteration of Hebrew and Yiddish (rule 43), Modern Greek (rule 11) and the Slavic languages (rule 10) may be obtained from the Library of Congress at small cost.
[3] Vatican 455.
[4] For a list of typographical characters and abbreviations most commonly used in 15th and 16th century books, see U.S. Govt. print. off., *Manual of foreign languages,* *op. cit.,* p.129-30.

? ? ?,
    Doit-on pleurer sa femme

卐
    The language of the stars

****
    Mémoires pour servir à l'histoire de la campagne de 1796

***, baron de
    Bibliographie des ouvrages de poésie...française

A B C book
Aagaard, Carl Johan
Alden, John
— — and ships and sealing wax
Andover

b) **Signs with letters** (used as author heading)

When a letter or a syllable is followed by signs, disregard the signs and arrange by the letter or letters. Subarrange as above.

M***
    Catalogue des livres choisis

M**
    Notices des livres du cabinet

M****, Madame la comtesse de
M****, Mademoiselle
M_____, Mr
M***, Monsieur
M., A.H.
M., M.W.
M***, Paul Hyppolite
M., V.A.
Ma, Yin Ch'u
Mabie, Mary Louise
Mac__, pseud., see MacManus, James
Mac, Reinhold
Macadam, Catharine
W*****e, H*n*y
W***in**on, G****

c) **Ampersand**

Alphabet the character "&" as "and," "et," "und," etc., according to the language used.

England and Canada
England & Germany
England and her colonies
Revue des questions historiques
Revue & examen des expositions nationales
Zur geschichte der costüme
Zur geschichte & charakteristik des deutschen genius

4. Initials

See also Abbreviations (Rule 5)

a) Arrange an initial before a word beginning with the same initial letter.

b) Arrange initials standing for names of organizations, broadcasting stations, airships, etc., whether punctuated or not, as initials and not as abbreviations, i.e., not as if spelled in full. For initials standing for geographical names, *see* Abbreviations (Rule 5: *a*).

c) When headings consist of initials only, arrange initials standing for authors' names, *if inverted* (e.g., A., F. P.), before initials that are not inverted.

```
A., A.,    see   Willis, Anthony Armstrong
A., B.
A., E.V.,   see   Trezavant, Eva Whitthorn
A., F.P.,   see   Adams, Franklin Pierce
A., T.,   see   Ashe, Thomas
A.A.,   see   Willis, Anthony Armstrong
A.A.A.,   see   U.S. Agricultural adjustment
     administration
A A C color photography
ABC of the NRA
A bas Rigolboche
ADAC — motorwelt
A.E.,   see   Russell, George William
A.E.F.,   see   U.S. Army. A.E.F., 1917-1920
     and also titles beginning A.E.F.
The A.E.F. in battle
A.L.A.   see   American library association;  Automobile
     legal association;  and also titles beginning A.L.A.
A.L.A. booklist
A.L.A... directory of tourist homes
A.L.A. in Siberia
A la mode cookery
A.S.M.E. news
A was an archer
Aa, Cornelis van der
Ambach, E. L.
American expeditionary force,   see   U.S.  Army.
     A.E.F., 1917-1920;  also titles beginning A.E.F.
American library association,   see also   titles begin-
     ning  A.L.A.
Automobile legal association,   see also   titles begin-
     ning  A.L.A.
```

This arrangement follows the general usage in regard to filing personal names (Rule 19). The *following alternative with its single alphabet is preferred by many libraries* on the ground that users of the catalog do not distinguish between inverted and noninverted initials.

d) ALTERNATIVE RULE: Arrange initials standing for authors'
names, whether inverted or not, alphabetically with initials standing
for organizations or beginning a title, disregarding the inversion and
punctuation.

```
A.A.,    see   Willis, Anthony Armstrong
A.A.A.,    see   U.S. Agricultural adjustment
     administration
AAA travel...
A A C color photographs
A., B.
ABC of the NRA
A bas Rigolboche
ADAC — motorwelt
A.E.,    see   Russell, George William
A.E.F.,    see   U.S. Army.  A.E.F., 1917-1920
     and also titles beginning A.E.F.
The A.E.F. in battle
A., E. V.,    see   Trezavant, Eva Whitthorn
A., F. P.,    see   Adams, Franklin Pierce
A.L.A.,    see   American library association;  Automobile
     legal association;  and also titles beginning A.L.A.
A.L.A. booklist
A.L.A... directory of tourist homes
A.L.A. in Siberia
A la mode cookery
A.S.M.E. news
A., T.,    see   Ashe, Thomas
A was an archer
Aa, Cornelis van der
Aabel, Marie
American expeditionary force,    see   U.S. Army.  A.E.F.,
     1917-1920;  also titles beginning A.E.F.
American library association,    see also   titles begin-
     ning A.L.A.
Automobile legal association,    see also   titles begin-
     ning A.L.A.
```

5. Abbreviations

See also Elisions (Rule 6); Initials (Rule 4)

a) Arrange abbreviations as if spelled in full; e.g., Dr., Mr., Mrs.,
Mlle., S., St., Ste., etc., as Doctor (or in German, Doktor), Mister,
Mistress, Mademoiselle, San or Sanctus, Saint, Sainte, etc. Also Ha
(Greek 'A) as Hagios. This includes initials and other abbreviations
used for geographical names; e.g., N.Y. as New York, Gt. Brit. as
Great Britain.

```
Colonel Carter
Col. Ross of Piedmont
Colonel Withersby's strike
Dr. Gratten
The doctor, his wife and the clock
```

```
Dr. Jekyll and Mr. Hyde
Mrs. Ames
Mistress and Maid
Mrs. Dane's defense
Mistress of Husaby
St. Petersburg
Saint Pierre
St. Vincent
Ste. Anne des Monts
Sainte Beuve
United States and war
U.S. army facts and insignia
U.S. camera magazine
United States daily
```

An explanatory reference should be made from the abbreviation to the full form whenever necessary.

```
Mrs.
    Entries beginning with Mrs. are filed as if
spelled Mistress
St.
    Entries beginning with St. are filed as if
spelled Saint
```

b) Disregard the abbreviations K., K.K., I., R., etc. (standing for Kaiserlich, Königlich, Imperiale, Reale, etc.) at the beginning of names of foreign learned academies, societies, etc., and arrange by the word following the abbreviation. The words for which these abbreviations stand are not familiarly known or spoken as part of the name.

In the names of English societies, Imperial and Royal are not to be disregarded.

```
Acadians
R. Accademia dei Lincei, Rome
Accidents
K. Akademie der wissenschaften, Berlin
Akenside, Mark
Hoepli, Ulrico
K.K. Hof- und staatsdruckerei, Austria,   see   Austria,
    KK. Hof- und staatsdruckerie
Hoffer, Andreas
Royal empire society, London
```

6. Elisions

See also Names with an elided prefix (Rule 13)

Arrange elisions as they are printed and not as if spelled in full. Treat as one word the contraction of two words resulting from an elision.

Exception: Foreign articles and prepositions with a final vowel elided are to be treated as separate words and not as contractions.

```
Bibliothèque d'anthropologie
Bibliothèque d'histoire
Bibliothèque de la révolution
Cap'n Eri
Capo d'anno
De l'intelligence
De la vida internacional
Flower o' the lily
Flower of destiny
Who is who in literature
Who'd be king
Whom the gods destroy
Who's who
Whose home is the wilderness
```

Note: Some libraries make no exception of elided articles and prepositions, but this is contrary to the usage of the foreign language itself.

7. Initial article

For names beginning with an article, *see* Names with a prefix (Rule 13) and Oriental names (Rule 14)

a) In alphabeting titles, disregard an initial article in the nominative case in all languages; but in foreign languages do not disregard initial articles in other than the nominative case, because such articles contain a prepositional element.[5]

b) In case the form of the indefinite article is the same as that of the numeral "one" (e.g., the French "un" or "une") care must be taken to distinguish the use, because the numeral is to be regarded in filing.

c) As initial articles, "de" (dialect for "the") and "ye" (Anglo-Saxon and early English form of "the") are to be disregarded; but "ye," the personal pronoun of the second person plural, is to be regarded.

```
Au temps des équipages
De la terre à la lune
De libris
Dem dichter in der fernen bild geblieben
The den
Den lieben süssen mädeln
Les déracinés
Des alten handwerks recht und gewohnheit
Du contrat social
Dublin
Eine von zu vielen     [numeral]
Un homme à la mer
Eine kleine gefälligkeit
Das kleine heldenbuch
De night in de front from Chreesmas
```

---

[5] For articles to be disregarded in filing, see U.S. Govt. print. off., *op. cit.*

```
Ye olde fire laddies
Un de Baumugnes   [numeral]
Ye that judge     [personal pronoun]
```

A table of initial articles to be disregarded in foreign languages will be found in Appendix II.

8. Punctuation marks. Possessive case, etc.

See also Inverted titles (Rule 37:f)

In alphabeting titles, disregard punctuation marks and the apostrophe. For an exception to this rule, *see* Periodicals (Rule 37:c).

```
Boy Scouts              Life; a book for a young man
Boycott                 Life — a bowl of rice
Boys' clubs             Life after death
Boy's King Arthur       Life — an obstacle race
Boys of '76             Life and art
A boy's town            Life, mind and spirit
```

9. Numerals

a) Arrange numerals in the titles of books as if spelled out in the language of the rest of the title. Spell numerals and dates as they are spoken, but omit the "and" in spoken numerals except at a decimal point between two digits and in mixed numbers.

Note: The omission of the "and" is recommended because spoken numerals are so taught in American public schools. Many libraries, however, prefer to retain the "and" because it usually appears on title pages where numerals are written out.

```
100 as one hundred (not as a hundred)
101 as one hundred one (not as one hundred and one)
1000 as one thousand
1500 as fifteen hundred (not as one thousand five hundred)
1812 as eighteen twelve, if a date; otherwise as eighteen
        hundred twelve (not as one thousand eight
        hundred twelve)
2,341,406 as two million, three hundred forty-one
        thousand, four hundred six
6½ as six and one half
.624 as six hundred twenty-four thousandths
600.024 as six hundred and twenty-four thousandths
```

This rule is not precise because numerals are not always spoken the same, but it is practical because to file each numeral as if spelled in full raises difficulties for users of the catalog who will look under the spoken word.

```
Acht tage auf ehrenwort
Achtundvierziger
1813; ein cyklus   [achtzehnhundert dreizehn]
1812; ein historischer roman   [achtzehnhundert zwölf]
Dix, Lester
1812   [dix huit cent deux]
```

```
1812 ouverture   [dix huit cent douze]
Les dix-sept ans de Marthe
100 jahre bauen und schauen   [ein hundert]
1500 facts and similes
4½ years in the Italy mission [four and one half]
1940 book of houses   [nineteen forty]
1914 diary            [nineteen fourteen]
1917 war tax guide    [nineteen seventeen]
One hundred and one famous poems
One hundred best books
100 bungalows
150 radio hook-ups    [one hundred fifty]
101 metal-working projects    [one hundred one]
One thousand and one illustrations
One thousand juvenile delinquents
1001 one minute stories      [one thousand one]
1600 business books
Sixteen years in Siberia
$1200 a year
2400 business books
Two thousand years ago
```

A table of numerals in foreign languages will be found in Appendix III.

b) Numerals at the beginning of such titles as "Annual report," "Course in," "Proceedings," "Report," etc., are to be arranged numerically and not alphabetically.

```
General account      not    First report
First report                Fourth report
Second report               General account
Fourth report               Second report
```

c) Numerals following headings that are otherwise identical usually indicate a numerical or chronological arrangement. (*See* Rule 38)

10. Words spelled in two ways

See also Hyphened and compound words (Rule 11); Names spelled differently (Rule 15)

a) When title headings begin with a word that may be spelled in two ways (e.g., Labor and Labour) choose one spelling according to an accepted authority and file all titles under this form. Refer from the other spelling.

```
Labor and administration
Labour and industry
LABOR AND LABORING CLASSES
Labor economics
Labour in the commonwealth
LABORATORIES
Laboulaye
Labour,  see  Labor
```

The following alternative arrangement is also an accepted practice but is not as easy to consult unless the user of the catalog knows the exact spelling.

b) ALTERNATIVE RULE: When title headings begin with a word that may be spelled in two ways, arrange according to the spelling of the title page. Refer from one spelling to the other.

```
Labor,   see also the spelling  Labour
LABOR AND LABORING CLASSES
Labor economics
LABORATORIES
Laboulaye
Labour,   see also the spelling  Labor
Labour and industry
Labour in the commonwealth
```

11. Hyphened and compound words

See also Compound names (Rules 12-13)

a) Arrange hyphened words as separate words.[6]

b) Arrange as one word compound words that are printed as one;[7] but if a compound word is printed sometimes as one word and sometimes as two words (or hyphened) choose one form according to accepted usage[8] and refer from the other form.

This rule may also apply to titles beginning with such a compound (e.g., Hand book, Hand-book, Handbook). If, however, it is preferred to arrange titles as printed, references should be made from one form to the other. (cf. Rule 10:*b*)

```
The book and its story
BOOK-BINDING, see BOOKBINDING
BOOK COLLECTING
Book-hunter
Book of animals
BOOK-PLATES
BOOKBINDING
BOOKPLATES, see BOOK-PLATES
```

c) Arrange as one word, words with a hyphened prefix such as anti-, co-, electro-, ex-, inter-, mid-, non-, pan-, post-, pre-, pro-, re-, trans-, tri-, etc.

```
ANTI LANGUAGE
ANTICHRIST
ANTI-INJUNCTION LAW, see INJUNCTIONS
ANTI-RENT TROUBLES, NEW YORK, 1839-1846
ANTISEMITISM, see JEWISH QUESTION
```

---

[6] Cutter 317.
[7] Cutter 316.
[8] A. M. Ball, *Compounding in the English language.* (N.Y.: H. W. Wilson, 1939.)

```
Anti-Semitism yesterday and tomorrow
ANTISLAVERY
Anti-slavery tracts
Cooperative marketing
Co-operative  movement
Inter arma
Interaction
Inter-America
Inter-collegiate association
Intercollegiate bureau
Pro patria
Proal, J.A.
Pro-British history text-books
Pro-musica quarterly
Pro-Palestine federation
```

12. Names compounded of two words

For the further arrangement of entries under compound personal names, *see* Rules 17:*b*, 18 and 20.

Arrange names consisting of two or more words, with or without a hyphen, as separate words.

This includes names beginning with New, Old, East, North, Saint, San, Santa, etc.

```
New Hampshire              St. Petersburg
The New republic           Saint Vincent
New thought                Sainte Beuve
New York                   Saintine
Newark                     San Francisco
North Africa               San Jose scale
North Haven                Sanborn
North Wales                Santa Lucia
Northampton                Santagnello
```

An *alternative* practice found in many reference books and in some libraries is to treat a name beginning with Saint, San, Santa, etc., as a name with a prefix (cf. Rule 13) and to file as one word. This practice is not recommended because Saint, San, etc., are words, not prefixes.

13. Names with a prefix

For Oriental names beginning with an article, *see* Rule 14:*a*.

a) Arrange a name with a prefix as one word.[9] This includes names in which an article or a preposition is written as part of the name and is not transposed; such names as Ap Thomas, D'Arcy, Des Barres, Du Challu, Fitz Allen, Le Sage, L'Estrange, MacFingal, O'Neal, Van Allen, Zum Felde, Zur Brücke, ZuTavern, etc.

---

[9] Cutter 311.

Defoe	Las Vegas, N.M.
De la Roche	L'Estrange, Alfred
Delaware	Le Strange, Guy
Del Mar	L'Estrange, Roger
DeMorgan	Los Angeles
El Dorado	Ocantus
Eldorado, Neb.	O'Casey
El Paso, Texas	Tenberg
Lasale	Ten Broeke
La Salle	Vancouver
Lassalle	Van Dyke

b) Names beginning with the prefix M' and Mc are filed as if spelled Mac, because they are so pronounced.[10]

An explanatory reference should be made from the abbreviated form to the full form, as

M' (or Mc)
    Names beginning with M' or Mc are filed as if spelled
    Mac

Mach	MacLaren, J.M.
McHale	M'Laren, J.T.
Machard	McLaren, L.L.
McHardy	MacLaren, R.S.

14. Oriental names

a) Mohammedan (Arabic, Persian, Turkish) and Hebrew names

(1) Disregard the initial article al- or el- (or the assimilated forms ad-, ar-, as-, az-) prefixed to Arabic, etc., names (e.g., al-Ghazzali) and the article ha- or he- prefixed to Hebrew names. But when the article comes between the parts of a name (e.g., 'Abd al Latīf) it is to be regarded.

(2) When a Mohammedan or Hebrew name begins with a part expressing relationship (e.g., the Arabic Abd, Abu, Ibn; the Hebrew Ab, Abi, Ben; the Syriac Bar) the parts are to be alphabeted as separate words.

This is the practice adopted by the Library of Congress and by a number of American universities and is recommended by the Oriental institute of the University of Chicago. European practice favors arranging as one word.

(Note: In the following examples, the names are not given in complete cataloging fullness, but in sufficient length to illustrate the rule.)

'Abd al-Ali
Abd al-Wāhid
'Abd Allāh, see also Abdallah
'Abd Allāh ibn Ahmad

---

[10] Cutter 312.

```
'Abd Allāh Sfer
Abdala
Abdalian
Abdallah,  see also  'Abd Allāh
Abū 'Abd Allāh Bahā
Abū 'Abd Allāh Muḥammad ibn Sa'd
Abū 'Abdallāh ibn Yakub
Abū 'Abdallāh Muḥammad ibn Muḥammad
Abū al-'Alā
Abū al-Faḍl
Abū al-Fidā
Abū al-Walīd
Abū 'Ali Jephet,  see  Japheth ben Eli
Abū Bakr
Abū Sa'īd
Abucacim
Abū'l-Fazl,  see  Abū al-Faḍl
Abūlafia, Abraham ben Samuel
Abulfeda,  see  Abū al-Fidā
Bar Ali
Bar-Am, Moshe
Bar-Hebraeus, Gregorius,  see  Gregorius,
   'Abū al-Faraj
Barabas, Béla
Ben Adhem
Ben Assher
Benade
Benassi
```

✓ b) Chinese names

Arrange Chinese names by the first part (family name) whether
it is separated by a comma or not. But an old Chinese name that
consists of only two hyphened syllables (e.g., Lao-tzŭ, "the Old one")
is to be filed as a two-word phrase.

```
Lao-tzŭ
Laos
Li Chang
Li, Chi
Li Chih-ch'ang
Li, Ching-chen
Li Hung-Chang
Li, Kung-lin, known as Li Lung-mien
Libby
Tai, Chi-t'ao
Tai, Tse Chien
Tai-ping rebellion
T'ai-Shang
Taine
```

Some libraries prefer to file a two-syllable hyphened name as one
word because it is sometimes written as one word. References should be
made from the name spelled as one word, e.g., Laotzŭ, *see* Lao-tzŭ.

15. Names spelled differently
Cf. Rule 13: *b*

Arrange separately names that differ in spelling however slightly. Refer from one spelling to the other.

```
Andersen,   see also the spelling Anderson,
     Anderssen,   Andersson
Andersen, Anders
Andersen, Hans Christian
Anderson,   see also the spellings etc.
Anderson, Arthur
Anderson, James
Anderssen,   see also the spellings etc.
Anderssen, Adolf
Anderssen, Walter
Andersson,   see also the spellings etc.
Andersson, Axel

Clark,   see also the spelling   Clarke
Clark, Allen Culling
Clark, Howard Walton
Clark university
Clarke, Adam
```

Note: In the case of forename entries where there is a slight difference of spelling in other than the first syllable, e.g., Catharine and Catherine, Elisabeth and Elizabeth, many libraries disregard the difference and file according to the more commonly used spelling, with reference from the other. *See* Catherine in the comprehensive example, Appendix V.

16.-18. FORENAME ENTRIES

The arrangement of common forename entries presents difficulties to the user of the catalog, who does not know the form of the distinguishing designation chosen by the cataloger nor by what part of the designation the forename is alphabeted. A wide diversity of practice in catalogs and reference books indicates that no simple or fully satisfactory method of solving this problem has been found. *Two orders of arrangement are offered:* by the first (Rule 17) forename entries are filed before surname entries of the same name; by the second (Rule 18) forename entries follow surname entries. *The former arrangement is the generally accepted practice in larger libraries;* the *latter arrangement* may be used by a library of any size but *is particularly recommended to smaller libraries* because its alphabetical order is more intelligible to the average reader.[11]

---

[11] Theresa Hitchler, *Cataloguing for small libraries*. Rev. ed. American library association, 1915. o.p. p.262-69.

16. Forename entries (general rules)

 a) Alphabet forenames that are the same by the designation or appellative following the name.

 b) Disregard a numeral following a forename except when necessary to distinguish between forenames with the same designation.

 c) In the names of sovereigns, disregard an epithet, such as "the Conqueror," "the Great," etc., when it comes between the forename and the designation. When the epithet is familiarly known, a reference should be made from the name alphabeted by the epithet, especially from the English form.[12]

```
Charles II, le Chauve, king of France
Charles IV, le Bel, king of France
Charles IX, king of France
Charles, the Bald, see Charles II, le Chauve,
    king of France
```

 d) Disregard a second forename that comes *between* a numeral and a designation; but if the second forename *precedes* the numeral, treat as a compound forename and do not disregard.

```
Karl IV, king of Sweden
Karl X Gustaf, king of Sweden
Karl XII, king of Sweden
Karl August, crown prince of Sweden
```

17. Forename entries. Arrangement 1 (Before surname)

Arrange a forename entry before a surname entry beginning with the same name.

 a) Arrange forenames that begin with the same name in two main groups as follows: —

> (1) Forenames followed by a designation of rank, office or other title, such as bishop, brother, emperor, king, prince, pope, saint, sister, etc. Arrange alphabetically by the word indicating rank, etc., disregarding articles and prepositions.
>
> (2) Forenames followed by an appellative (epithet, byname, descriptive word or phrase used for identification, e.g., Thomas, *Anglo-Norman poet*, Thomas, *of Edessa*, Thomas *Spalatensis*) and forenames compounded of two or more words, the second part of which may be a second forename (e.g., Mary Clare), a family name (e.g., Mary Stuart), a name derived from a place (e.g., Charles d'Or-

---

[12] The practice of the *A.L.A. cataloging rules* and of the Library of Congress in inserting epithets between the names of sovereigns and their titles, makes such a reference puzzling to the user of the catalog. The awkwardness can be avoided by placing the epithet in curves after the title; e.g., Charles, duke of Burgundy (le Téméraire), William I, king of England (the Conqueror).

léans), or a phrase (e.g., Mary of the Visitation). Interfile forenames followed by appellatives alphabetically with compound forenames, having regard to all words, articles and prepositions included.

Note: Library of Congress prints appellatives in italics, and all parts of a compound name is bold-faced type. Disregard typography in filing.

```
John (forename)
  John, abbot of Ford
  John, Brother
  John III, duke of Brabant, see Jean III, etc.
  John, the Fearless, duke of Burgundy, see Jean,
    sans Peur, etc.
  John, [father]
  John, king of England
  John III Sobieski, king of Poland, see Jan III, etc.
  John II, king of Portugal, see Joao II, etc.
  John XIII, pope
  John XXI, pope
  John, Prester
  John, Saint, apostle
  John, son of Sabanis
John (compound, etc.; forenames)
  John de Burgh, see Burgo, Joannes de
  John Gabriel
  John of Austria
  John, of Damascus, Saint, see Joannes, etc.
  John, of Gaddesden
  John of Gaunt, duke of Lancaster
  John of Lancaster, duke of Bedford
  John, of Nepomuk, Saint, see Jan, etc.
  John of the Cross, Saint, see Juan de la Cruz, Saint
  John of Wales
  John, the Baptist
  John, the Fearless, see Jean, sans Peur, duke of
    Burgundy
  John, the Painter
  John Wallensis, see John of Wales
John (surname)
  John, Alois
John (titles, etc.)
  John and Joan
  John of Bordeaux (Old play)
```

Additional examples under Charles, Mary and Thomas will be found in Appendix I.

The above arrangement is recommended (1) because the alphabetic order of rank is to be preferred to the Cutter (302) classed order, as simpler for the user of the catalog to whom the order of classes is not self-evident; and (2) because compound forenames are not, in many cases, distinguishable in form from single forenames with an appellative.

For libraries that prefer to retain the Cutter arrangement and a separate filing of compound forenames, the following rule is given: —

b) ALTERNATIVE RULE (Cutter order) : Arrange entries of a common forename in the following order: —

(1) Saints; arranged alphabetically by designation.
(2) Popes; arranged numerically.
(3) Sovereigns; arranged alphabetically by country. (Include queen consorts in this group.)
(4) Princes and noblemen; arranged by chief word in title, disregarding articles, prepositions and the word indicating rank.
(5) Others; arranged alphabetically by appellative or designation having regard to all words, articles and prepositions included.
(6) Arrange compound forenames beginning with the same name after the single forenames. Arrange alphabetically, having regard to all words, articles and prepositions included.

```
John (Saints)
   John,  Saint,  apostle
   John, of Damascus,  Saint,  see  Joannes, etc.
   John, of Nepomuk,  Saint, see  Jan,  etc.
John (Popes)
   John XIII,  pope
   John XXI,  pope
John (Sovereigns)
   John,  king of England
   John III, Sobieski, king of Poland,  see  Jan III,  etc.
   John II,  king of Portugal,  see  Joao II,  etc.
John (Noblemen)
   John III,  duke of Brabant,  see  Jean III,  etc.
   John, the Fearless,  duke of Burgundy,  see  Jean,
      sans Peur,  etc.
John (Others)
   John,  abbot of Ford
   John,  Brother
   John,  father
   John,  of Gaddesden
   John,  of Salisbury,  bp. of Chartres
   John  of Wales
   John,  Prester
   John,  son of Sabanis
   John the Baptist
   John, the Painter,  see  Aitken, James
   John Wallensis,  see  John of Wales
```

```
John (compound forenames)
    John de Burgh,  see  Burgo, Joannes de
    John Gabriel, sister
    John of Austria,  see  Juan de Austria
    John of Gaunt,  duke of Lancaster
    John of Lancaster,  duke of Bedford
    John of the Cross,  Saint,  see  Juan de la Cruz,  Saint
John (surname)
    John, Alois
John (titles, etc.)
    John and Joan
    John of Bordeaux (Old play)
```

Note 1: Linderfelt (397) calls for more classes, viz., (1) Saints, (2) Popes, (3) Emperors, (4) Kings, (5) Sovereign princes, (6) Other princes of sovereign houses, (7) Noblemen, (8) Others. Library practice varies as to the number of classes.

Note 2: Some libraries arrange compound forenames after the single forenames in the class to which each belongs.

18. Forename entries. Arrangement 2 (After surname)

Arrange a forename entry after the surname entries of the same name, interfiling with titles and other headings beginning with the same word. Include compound forename entries. Alphabet with regard to all words, articles and prepositions included.

Additional examples under Mary and Thomas will be found in Appendix I.

```
Charles  (surname)
    Charles, David
    Charles, William
    Charles-Roux, François*
Charles  (forenames, titles, etc.)
    Charles  [a title]
    Charles Alexander,  duke of Lorraine
    Charles,  archduke of Austria,  see  Karl, etc.
    Charles Auchester, a novel
    Charles Borromeo,  Saint,  see  Carlo Borromeo,  Saint
    Charles City, Iowa
    Charles,  count of Angoulême, duke of Orléans,  see
        Charles d'Orléans
    Charles,  count of Valois
    Charles d'Orléans
    Charles de Lorraine,  duke of Lower Lorraine
    Charles de Saint Paul,  see  Vialart, Charles,  bp.
    Charles Dickens in London
    Charles,  duke of Burgundy (le Téméraire)
    Charles II,  duke of Lorraine
    Charles,  duke of Orléans, count of Angoulême,  see
        Charles d'Orléans
    Charles Emanuel I,  duke of Savoy,  see  Carlo
        Emanuele I, etc.
```

```
Charles V,  emperor of Germany,  see  Karl V, etc.
Charles family
Charles II,  king of France (le Chauve)
Charles, king of the Franks,  see  Charlemagne
Charles II,  king of Great Britain
Charles, le Chauve,  see  Charles II,  king of France
     (le Chauve)
Charles, le Téméraire,  see  Charles,  duke of Burgundy
     (le Téméraire)
Charles Louis de Bourbon,  duke of Parma
Charles Martel,  mayor of the palace
The Charles men
Charles,  père
Charles, the Bald,  see  Charles II,  king of France
     (le Chauve)
Charles, the Bold,  see  Charles,  duke of Burgundy
     (le Téméraire)
Charles, the Great,  see  Charlemagne
Charles the Second,  a play
```

*If Rule 20:b is adopted, this compound surname will file with the forenames, titles, etc.

19. Surname entries

Arrange headings of the same surname as follows: —

a) A surname alone or followed only by an appellative or a designation (descriptive phrase, title of honor, etc.) precedes the same surname with initials or forenames.

b) A surname followed by an initial precedes the same surname followed by a fully written-out forename beginning with the same initial letter.

c) When both surnames and forenames are the same, arrange chronologically by date of birth, if known; otherwise by date of death or by period as given in the heading.

d) A name without date precedes the same name with dates. Arrange the names without date by the distinguishing designation following the name.

e) A pseudonym files after a real name alone, but before the same name followed by dates. It interfiles alphabetically with other designations.

f) Disregard titles of honor and distinction such as Capt., Dr., Hon., Lady, Mlle., Mme., Mrs., Sir, etc., before a name and Bp., D.D., F.R.S., LL.D., baron, comte, graf, etc., after a name, unless it is necessary to distinguish between names that would otherwise be identical.

```
Brown, ---
Brown, Capt.
Brown, Mrs.
Brown, pseud.
Brown, A. G.
```

```
Brown, Albert
Brown, Mrs. Augusta
Brown, B. L.
Brown, John
Brown, John,  genealogist
Brown, John,  of Great Yarmouth
Brown, John,  philomath
Brown, John,  pseud.
Brown, Sir John
Brown, John, 1716-1766
Brown, John,  d. 1811
Brown, John, 1810-1882
Brown, John A
Brown, Sir John Abercrombie
Brown, John Allen
Brown, Peter,  fl. 1776
Brown, Peter,  1764-1863
Brown, R. A.
Brown, R. Grant
Brown, Ralph
Browne, Charles Albert
```

20. Surname entries—Compound surnames

a) Arrange surnames compounded of two or more words after the simple surname, but before titles and other headings beginning with the same word.

```
Hall, William
Hall-Quest, Alfred
Hall-Wood, Mary
Hall & Patterson
HALL FAMILY
HALL MARKS
HALL OF FAME
```

The above rule is based on Cutter (313). If a straight alphabetical order is preferred, adopt the following alternative:—

b) ALTERNATIVE RULE: Arrange personal surnames compounded of two or more words after the simple surname, interfiled in alphabetical order with titles and other headings beginning with the same word.

```
Hall, William
Hall & Patterson
HALL FAMILY
HALL MARKS
HALL OF FAME
Hall-Quest, Alfred
Hall-Wood, Mary
Hallam, Arthur
```

21. Names of clan, family, house, dynasty, etc.

a) Interfile a surname followed by "clan," "family," "House of,"

"Dukes of," etc., alphabetically with the titles and other entries following the simple surname. Disregard an inversion.

Compound surnames followed by "family," etc., follow their specific form of name.

Lloyd, William	Medici, Lorenzo de', il
Lloyd George, David	Magnifico
LLOYD GEORGE FAMILY	Medici, Michele
Lloyd-Williams, Richard	Medici-Tornaquinci, Alfonso
Lloyd brothers, Cincinnati	Cosimo de'
LLOYD FAMILY	Medici antiqui omnes
Lloyd guide to Australia	MEDICI, HOUSE OF
Lloyd library	

b) ALTERNATIVE RULE: If Rule 20:*b* has been adopted, the order
of entries will vary slightly, as follows: —

Lloyd, William	Medici, Lorenzo de'
Lloyd brothers, Cincinnati	Medici, Michele
LLOYD FAMILY	Medici antiqui omnes
Lloyd George, David	MEDICI, HOUSE OF
LLOYD GEORGE FAMILY	Medici-Tornaquinci, Alfonso
Lloyd guide to Australia	Cosimo de'
Lloyd library	
Lloyd-Williams, Richard	

22. Firm names

a) Arrange the name of a firm in which forenames or initials
follow the first name in its alphabetical place among the personal names.

Arrange a firm name without forename, a compound firm name,
or a phrase firm name, alphabetically with the titles and other headings
following the same name as surname.

```
Fraser, Alice
Fraser, Arthur, 1893-
Fraser, Arthur, and company
Fraser, Charles
Fraser, William
Fraser-Knight, James
Fraser & Charles
FRASER FAMILY
Fraser, firm, booksellers, London
The Fraser murder case
Fraser, Smith & co.
```

b) ALTERNATIVE RULE: If Rule 20:*b* has been adopted, the order
of entries will vary slightly as follows:

```
Fraser, Alice
Fraser, Arthur, 1893-
Fraser, Arthur, and company
Fraser, Charles
Fraser, William
```

```
Fraser & Charles
FRASER FAMILY
Fraser, firm, booksellers, London
Fraser-Knight, James
The Fraser murder case
Fraser, Smith & co.
```

23. Nobleman's title and bishop's see

Arrange a nobleman's title under which entry is made, and the name of a bishop's see from which reference is made to the family name, among personal names and not with places.

```
Holland, Edward James
Holland, Henry Fox,  1st baron
Holland, Henry Scott
Holland (Province)

London, Alfred
London, Arthur, bp. of, see Winnington-Ingram, Arthur
     Foley, bp. of London
London, Jack
London, Conn.
```

24. Order of entries

A dictionary catalog theoretically consists of author, subject and title entries interfiled to form a single alphabet; but in actual practice, when the same heading is used for the three kinds of entry, the strictly alphabetic order has been broken down into more or less complex classed arrangements. This tendency, in some cases, has been carried to an extreme which renders a card catalog unnecessarily difficult to consult. In recent years there has been a reaction in favor of a more nearly alphabetic arrangement. Two orders of arrangement are, therefore, outlined below and are fully explained and illustrated in the rules and examples for arrangement under Place (Rules 31-32), Subject (Rules 33-35) and Title (Rule 37). Both arrangements are in use in libraries of different types and different sizes and both are equally recommended.

The first arrangement, designated as the Classed order, is based on Cutter (300) and has long been in general use, although in its application the Cutter rule has been variously interpreted, amplified and modified.

The second arrangement is designated as the Alphabetic order, because it retains an alphabetic arrangement wherever practicable.

    a) Classed order
        (1) When the same word, or combination of words, is used as the heading of different kinds of entry, adopt the fol-

lowing order: person, place, subject (other than person
or place), title.

(2) Subject entries under a personal or corporate name are
to be filed immediately after the author entries for the
same name.

(3) Subdivisions under person, place or subject file after the
person, place or subject without subdivision and before
other headings beginning with the same word.

```
Love (person)
    Love, John L.
    LOVE, JOHN L.
    Love, William
LOVE (subject)
    LOVE
    LOVE — POETRY, see  LOVE POETRY
    LOVE — QUOTATIONS, MAXIMS, ETC.
    LOVE (IN THEOLOGY)
Love (titles, etc.)
    Love
    Love and beauty
    Love-letters
    LOVE POETRY
    Love songs, old and new

Baltimore (person)
    Baltimore, Frederick Calvert,  7th baron
Baltimore (place: author)
    Baltimore
    BALTIMORE — Board of health
    BALTIMORE — BOARD OF HEALTH
    Baltimore — Fire dept.
BALTIMORE (place: subject)
    BALTIMORE
    BALTIMORE — DESCRIPTION
    BALTIMORE — HISTORY
    BALTIMORE, OHIO [another place]
Baltimore (titles, etc.)
    Baltimore American
    BALTIMORE CO., MD.
    Baltimore, past and present
```

b) Alphabetic order

(1) When the same word, or combination of words, is used as
the heading of different kinds of entry, arrange the entries
alphabetically by the word following the entry word. Disregard kind of entry and form of heading, *except* as
follows: —

(2) Arrange personal surnames before the other entries beginning with the same word.

This almost universal practice is adopted for practical convenience because users of the catalog may not know the designation or forename of the person sought and are confused and annoyed at having to search through so many entries that are not personal names.

Note: Small libraries may prefer to interfile personal names also.[13]

(3) Subject entries under a personal or corporate name are to be filed immediately after the author entries for the same name.

(4) When title and subject headings are identical, file the title entries after the subject entries.

This segregation of title entries facilitates the search for a title when the author is not known, especially when the subject entries are numerous. In order that the title entries may not be overlooked, a guide-card should be used.

When, however, subject entries are few or the subject is a place, the title entries may be interfiled with the subject entries, arranging by the main heading of the book. This practice is recommended to small libraries. (cf. Rule 32:c)

```
Love, John L
LOVE, JOHN L
Love, William
LOVE
Love
Love and beauty
LOVE (IN THEOLOGY)
Love-letters
A love match
LOVE POETRY
LOVE — QUOTATIONS, MAXIMS, ETC.
Love songs, old and new

Baltimore, Frederick Calvert,  7th baron
Baltimore American
Baltimore and Ohio magazine
BALTIMORE CO., MD.
Baltimore, Md.14
BALTIMORE, MD.
Baltimore. Md.  Board of health
BALTIMORE, MD.  BOARD OF HEALTH
BALTIMORE, MD. — DESCRIPTION
Baltimore, Md.  Fire dept.
BALTIMORE, MD. — HISTORY
Baltimore, Ohio
Baltimore, past and present
Baltimore weekly magazine
```

---

[13] S. G. Akers, *Simple library cataloging* (Chicago: American library association, 1927), p.70.
[14] The name of the state has to be inserted to maintain the alphabetic order. (*See* Rule 32:d Note)

25.-26. ARRANGEMENT UNDER AUTHOR

Rule 25 covers the general alphabetic arrangement of entries under an author's name.

When, however, under a classic or voluminous author, the alphabetic order becomes difficult to consult because of the number of titles, editions, translations, etc., a grouping of entries should be introduced. Rule 26: *a* offers a simple grouped arrangement, adapted to the use of public libraries, which may be adopted, in part or in whole, as the need arises. Rules 26: *b* and 26: *c* outline alternative arrangements for university and large reference collections, where a more detailed grouped order, with subarrangement primarily by date, is usually required.

25. General arrangement under author

Under an author's name, personal or corporate, arrange the entries in two files: (*a*) works by the author, (*b*) works about the author.

a) Works *by* the author

(1) Arrange in one file all the entries, both main and secondary, for a person as author, joint author, compiler, editor, illustrator, translator and general added entry. Subarrange alphabetically by the title of the book.

Note: An earlier practice, still followed in some libraries, is to arrange the secondary author entries in a separate alphabet after the main author entries. This practice is not recommended because users of the catalog overlook entries so filed.

(2) In interfiling the secondary author entries with the main author entries, disregard the main author heading on the secondary entry cards and subarrange by title. To make this clear, underline the word in the title by which the entry is subarranged, or line out the main entry heading.

Optional exception: When a secondary entry is the editor or translator of another person's work, especially in the case of classic authors, subarrange by the main author heading instead of by the title. But do not do so if the editor or translator may be looked for as the author of the book either because of the wording or typography of the title page or because the editorial work is as important as the text. Since this is a matter of judgment, the filing should be clearly indicated by the cataloger.

(3) At the beginning of a title the author's name, even in the possessive case, may be disregarded; but not if it forms an integral part of the title.

```
Cicero
   (Ciceron.) L'amitié
   (Cicero's) Offices
   (Cicero:) select orations
   (Cicero's) selected orations
Shakespeare
   (Shakespeare's) As you like it
   (Shakespeare's) historical plays
   Shakespeare adaptations
   Shakespeare's genius
```

(4) Analytics: Alphabet an author analytic by the title of the analytic, not by the title of the book. If there are two analytics of the same title subarrange by the main entry of the book.

If the title of an analytic and of a separate work are the same, file the separate work first, disregarding a subtitle or a second title, if any.

```
O'Neill
   The emperor Jones, Different, The straw
O'Neill
   The emperor Jones  (In Church.  Curtain!)
O'Neill
   The emperor Jones  (In Locke.  Plays of Negro
      life)
```

Note: It is clearer if the title as well as the author of the analytic is typed in the heading. Otherwise the analytic title should be underlined where it appears on the card.

(5) Criticisms: File a criticism of a particular title, edition, or translation, immediately after the entry for that title, edition or translation.

(6) Editions: Editions of the same title may be variously arranged depending partly on the character of the material and partly on the type of library to be served.

For scientific, technical and other factual material, arrangement by date is usually important. The latest edition may be filed first by arranging the dates in reverse order.

For belles-lettres, arrangement by publisher, editor, translator, or illustrator is to be preferred in public libraries. Editions, with or without editor, when better known by series (e.g., Loeb classics), should be arranged by series. Arrangement by date better meets the needs of university libraries, but may be used wherever preferred. (Cf. Rule 26: *b*)

Editions arranged by date only, should precede editions arranged by publisher, editor, etc.

Editions of the same title and same publisher or editor are subarranged by date.

Variations in subtitle may usually be disregarded.

McPherson
A course in general chemistry. 4th ed.   1936
———   2d ed.   1921
———   1915
———   1913

Stevenson
A child's garden of verses, N.Y., Appleton, 1923
———   N.Y., Crowell, c1918
———   Cambridge, Eng., Heffer, 1922
——— illus. by Burd   Akron, O., Saalfield, 1929
———   N.Y., Scribner, 1909
——— with illus. by Smith. N.Y., Scribner, 1930
——— illus. by Noé   N.Y., Sears
——— ; introd. and notes by Weekes. Philadelphia,
                                  Winston, 1928

Note: The Stevenson example shows arrangement by publisher. Arrangement by illustrator is shown in the Lang example following; by editor in the examples under Rule 26.

(7) Translations: Either of the following arrangements may be used. The second is suitable for large collections and for voluminous authors.

(a) Arrange each translation alphabetically by its own title. A note under the English title may be used to refer to the title under other languages, if needed.

Maeterlinck
  Der blaue vogel
Maeterlinck
  The blue bird
      The library has this book also in French
  (L'oiseau bleu) and in German (Der blaue vogel)
Maeterlinck
  Death
Maeterlinck
  Monna Vanna
Maeterlinck
  La mort
Maeterlinck
  L'oiseau bleu

(b) ALTERNATIVE RULE: Arrange translations alphabetically by *language* immediately after the original title. The original title and the language of the translation should appear in the heading of the card. Refer from the title of the translation.

(For an alternative arrangement see Rule 26:c)

```
Maeterlinck
  The blue bird
      Translations are filed alphabetically by
      language after the original title:
      L'oiseau bleu
Maeterlinck
  La mort
Maeterlinck      (La mort. English)
  Death
Maeterlinck
  L'oiseau bleu
Maeterlinck      (L'oiseau bleu. English)
  The blue bird
Maeterlinck      (L'oiseau bleu. German)
  Der blaue vogel
```

(*Note:* Only one reference is shown in the above examples.)

b) Works *about* the author

   (1) Arrange in a second file the entries for works about
   the author, alphabeting by the main entry of the book;
   or, if an analytic, by the author of the analytic.
   Exception: The subject entry for a criticism of an individual title files immediately after the author entries
   for the title (cf. *a* 5 preceding).

   (2) Arrange subject subdivisions alphabetically by the subdivision. (*See* examples under Rule 26)

```
Lang, Andrew
  Adventures among books

  Lang, Andrew,  ed.
Lang, Mrs Leonora Blanche
  Book of saints and heroes

Lang, Andrew
  Complete works

Lang, Andrew
  Homer and the epic

  Lang, Andrew,  tr.
Homerus
  The Iliad

Lang, Andrew
  Late Jacobite tracts (In Bibliographica...)

Lang, Andrew
  The Maid of France
      The library has this title also in
      French (La Pucelle de France)

Lang, Andrew
  The making of religion
```

    LANG, ANDREW
        THE MAKING OF RELIGION
Tyrrell, George
    The faith of the millions,   v.2

    Lang, Andrew, tr.
Homerus
    The Odyssey

Lang, Andrew
    La Pucelle de France

Lang, Andrew, ed.
    The red fairy book... with numerous illus. by
        A.J. Ford and Lancelot Speed. London, Long-
        mans, 1890

    _____, with illus. by M. DeV. Lee. Philadel-
        phia, Macrae Smith, [1927]

    _____; introd. and notes by M.D. Holmes, illus.,
        by Frederick Richardson. Philadelphia, Wins-
        ton, [1930]

    _____, illus. by Gustaf Tenggren. Philadelphia,
        McKay, 1924

    Lang, Andrew, jt. auth.
Haggard, Sir H.R.
    The world's desire
    LANG, ANDREW
Gordon, G.S.
    Andrew Lang
    LANG, ANDREW
Rait, R.S.
    Andrew Lang as historian

If the optional exception (*a* 2) is adopted, the order of entries
would vary as follows:—

    Lang, Andrew
        Adventures among books

    Lang, Andrew
        Complete works

    Lang, Andrew
        Homer and the epic

    Lang, Andrew, tr.
    Homerus
        The Iliad

    Lang, Andrew, tr.
    Homerus
        The Odyssey

    Lang, Andrew, ed.
Lang, Mrs Leonora Blanche
    Book of saints and heroes

Lang, Andrew
    The making of religion

> Lang, Andrew, jt. auth.
> Haggard, <u>Sir</u> R.H.
> The <u>w</u>orld's desire

For an arrangement under Shakespeare, *see* the Comprehensive example, Appendix V.

26. Special arrangement under classic and voluminous authors

It is difficult for users of the catalog to locate a specific title, edition or translation under a classic author in even a medium-sized collection, therefore great care should be taken that guide-cards indicate clearly the grouping and arrangement of entries. Notes on the guide-cards should explain the order and method of alphabeting within each group.

a) Arrangement 1

Arrange entries in the following main groups: (1) Complete, or nearly complete, works, (2) Selected works, Selections, etc., (3) Single works, (4) Works about the author.

(1) Complete works

Disregard wording of title and arrange by editor; or, if no editor, by series or publisher if well-known, otherwise by date. (cf. Rule 25:*a* 5-7)

(2) Selected works (partial collections, collected fragments and spurious works). Selections (anthologies, quotations, etc.). Arrange by *title* and subarrange according to Rule 25:*a.*

Note 1: When the title of a partial collection, consisting of two or more works, begins with the title of the first work (e.g., Cicero, De senectute et De amicitia), the entry is probably better filed with the entries for the first work under *Single* works, disregarding the other titles in the entry. Added entry may be made for the other title or titles.

Note 2: Selections (anthologies, extracts, quotations and other miscellanea) may, if preferred, form a separate group arranged before or after *Single* works.

(3) Single works (including fragments of a single work and single spurious or attributed works)

Arrange alphabetically by the best-known title in the original language.[15] Indicate the titles by guide-cards and refer from other forms of the title and from well-known forms of the English title.

Under each title subarrange the entries like *Complete* works.

---

[15] It is suggested that the Library of Congress Classification schedules for class P-PZ (Literature) be used to establish the original titles.

Note: For public libraries, arrangement under the best known English title may be preferred, with reference from the original title; e.g., under Cicero use the title Friendship and refer from Amicitia, De amicitia, Laelius.

(4) Works about the author
See Rule 25: *b*

Cicero. <u>Complete works</u>. <u>Latin text</u>
    Arranged by editor, series or pubisher, disregarding wording of title.

Opera; ed. stereotypa		1816-22?
Opera.	Baiter	1860-69
M. Tullii Ciceronis opera.	Ernesti	1810
M. Tullii Ciceronis opera omnia.	Ernesti	1819
Opera.	Gronovius	1692
Scripta quae manserunt omnia.	Klotz	1855-83
M. Tullii Ciceronis opera.	Lallemand	1768
Opera.	Olivet	1758

Cicero. <u>Complete works</u>. (<u>Translations</u>)
    Arranged by language and under language by translator.

The works of Cicero	English	
Oeuvres...	French	Du Ryer
Oeuvres complètes...	French and Latin[16]	Nisard
Oeuvres complètes...	French	Prévost

Cicero. <u>Selected works</u>. <u>Selections, etc</u>. (<u>Latin text</u>)
    Arranged by title
Ars oratorio; selections
Cicero's correspondence
Cicero's idioms
De officiis; De amicitia; De senectute; Paradoxa...[17]
Eleven orations of Cicero
EPISTOLAE
    Boot. Observationes criticae
Epistolae ad familiares
EPISTOLAE AD FAMILIARES. 1474
    Scholderer. A supposed Foligno edition of 1474
(Cicero's) essays on old age and friendship; and
      Cicero's Oration for Milo
Extracts from Cicero
Offices, essays and letters of Cicero
Orationes et epistolae selectae
Orations; ed. by Moore
Orations; ed. by Yonge
Select orations and letters
(Cicero): ten orations and selected letters
Thesaurus

Cicero. <u>Selected works</u>. <u>Selections</u>. (<u>Translations</u>)
    Arranged by language and under language by translator.[18]

---

[16] May be arranged with original texts, if preferred.
[17] May file among Single works under first title, if preferred.
[18] May file by title under language, if preferred.

```
Cicero's essays on Old age and Friend-
     ship; also his Paradoxes            English   Edmonds
Cicero's three books of offices; also
     his Cato major... [etc.]            English   Edmonds
Letters to several of his friends       English   Melmoth
Letters to his friends (Loeb classics) English   Williams
Lettres de Cicéron à ses amis  French and Latin  Prévost
```

Cicero. Single works
```
Academica (Academicae quaestiones)
Amicitia,  see  Laelius
Ars rhetorica,  see  Rhetorica
Brutus (De claris oratoribus)
Cato major de senectute.  (Latin text)
   Laelius et Cato major
   De senectute; dialogue on old age   Allen
   Caxton: Tulle Of olde age           Caxton & Sussebach
   Cato major de senectute.  Laelius   Crowell
   De senectute et De amicitia         Dillaway
   Cato major de senectute             Huxley
   Cato major et Laelius               Stickney
Cato major de senectute.   (Translations)
   Arranged by language and under language by translator.
   A defense of old age...             English   Houghton
   Cato major; or A discourse on
        old age...                      English   Logan
   Cato, or An essay on old age...      English   Melmoth
Consolatio
De amicitia,  see  Laelius
De claris oratoribus,  see  Brutus
De consolatione,  see  Consolatio
De fato
De finibus bonorum et malorum
De inventione rhetorica,  see  Rhetorica
De officiis
   De officiis.  Atzert
   De officiis; tr... M'Cartney
DE OFFICIIS
   Adams.  De officiis et paradoxa
   Nelson.  De officiis in Christian thought
De senectute,  see  Cato major
Dream of Scipio,  see  Somnium Scipionis
Friendship,  see  Laelius
Laelius de amicitia
Laelius et Cato major                   1854
De senectute et De amicitia             Crowell
Laelius de amicitia                      Reid
Cato major et Laelius                    Stickney
Laelius; a dialogue on friendship        Shuckburgh
Officia,  see  De officiis
Old age,  see  Cato major
On friendship,  see  Laelius
On old age,  see  Cato major
Rhetorica
```

Somnium Scipionis
  Conway. From Orpheus to Cicero

CICERO. <u>Works about</u>
  Boissier
    Cicero and his friends
  Conway
    Makers of Europe
      Caesar the destroyer. <u>The originality of Cicero</u>.
  Peterson
    Cicero, a biography

    CICERO — BIBLIOGRAPHY
    CICERO — LANGUAGE

Shakespeare. <u>Complete works</u> (Includes complete dramatic
    works)
    Arranged by editor, etc., disregarding wording of title.
  Shakespeare's comedies, histories and tragedies. 1623
    (repr.1902)
  Mr William Shakespeare's comedies, histories and
    tragedies. 1632 (repr.1909)
  Complete works. 1905?
  <u>B</u>ell's edition of Shakespeare
  The family Shakespeare, ed. by <u>B</u>owdler
  Complete works, ed. by <u>C</u>raig. (Oxford Shakespeare)[19]
  Oxford Shakespeare; the complete works, ed. by <u>C</u>raig[20]
  Works... ed. by <u>G</u>ollancz. (Temple Shakespeare)[19]
  Pictorial edition... ed. by <u>K</u>night. 1839-43
  <u>K</u>nights cabinet edition... 1851
  Pictorial edition... ed. by <u>K</u>night. 2d rev. ed. 1867

Shakespeare. <u>Complete works</u>. (<u>Translations</u>)
    Arranged by language and under language by translator.

Shakespeare'n draamoja	Finnish	Cajender
Oeuvres dramatiques	French	Duval
Oeuvres complètes	French	Guizot
Shakespeare's dramatische werke	German	Schlegel

Shakespeare. <u>Poetical works</u>. (<u>Collected and Selected</u>)
    For the Sonnets alone, and for single poems (e.g., Venus and
    Adonis) *see* the file of *Single works*. Collections and selections of
    the poems are arranged by title.
  A book of Shakespeare's songs
  Poems. (Ariel edition)
  Poems; ed. by Brooke
  Poetical works of Shakespeare and Jonson
  Songs and sonnets; ed. by Palgrave
  Songs and sonnets; illus. by Robinson
  Songs from the plays
  Under the greenwood tree; songs from the plays

---

[19] May be arranged by series, if preferred.
[20] May be arranged by "Oxford," if preferred.

Shakespeare. <u>Poetical</u> <u>works</u>. (<u>Translations</u>)
    Arranged by language and under language by translator.
    Poems et sonnets   French   Lafond

Shakespeare. <u>Poetical</u> <u>works</u>. (<u>Criticism</u>)
    Lloyd, W.W. Critical essays on the lays of Shakespeare

Shakespeare. <u>Selected</u> <u>works</u>. <u>Selections</u>, <u>etc</u>.
    Arranged by title.
    For selections from the poetical works, *see* the file of *Poetical*
    works preceding.
    Aphorisms from Shakespeare
    The beauties of Shakespeare
    The children's Shakespeare
    Comedies; ed. by Craig
    Doubtful plays
    Five plays of Shakespeare
    Longman's school Shakespeare
    The masques of Psyche [<u>scenes</u>]
    Shakespeare adaptations
    Shakespeare apocrypha
    A Shakespeare festival [<u>a</u> <u>secondary</u> <u>entry</u> <u>with</u> <u>main</u>
      <u>entry</u> <u>under</u> <u>Simons</u>]
    Shakespearean comedies; ed. by Hale
    Tragedies; ed. by Craig
    The will

Shakespeare. <u>Selected</u> <u>works</u>. (<u>Translations</u>)
    Arranged by language.
    Shakespeare anthologie   German
    Dramas [4 plays]; tr. by Moratín   Spanish

Shakespeare. <u>Single</u> <u>works</u>
    Arranged under each work by editor, series, etc., disregarding the
    wording of the title.[21]
    As you like it
      As you like it; ed. by Darton (Bankside edition)[22]
      As you like it.   (Ben Greet Shakespeare)
      Shakespeare's As you like it Cooper
      The comedy of As you like it (Eclectic classics)
      Shakespeare's comedy of As
          you like it   Rolfe
    As you like it (<u>Translations</u>)
      A piacer vostro   Italian
    Catharine and Petruchio, <u>see</u> <u>his</u> Taming of the shrew
    Edward III, <u>see</u> Edward III (Drama)
    Hamlet
      Shakespeare's tragedy of Hamlet
    Henry IV, <u>see</u> <u>his</u> King Henry IV
    Julius Caesar
      The plays of Shakespeare. The tragedy of Julius
        Caesar

---

[21] Arrangement by title can be used, if preferred.
[22] Arranged by edition because better known, but arrangement by editor would also be correct.

King Henry IV
  King Henry the Fourth
King Henry IV, part 1
  The historie of Henrie the Fourth. Part 1
King Henry IV, part 2
  The second part of King Henry the Fourth
King Henry IV, part 2 (Translations)
  Enrico IV (parte seconda) tr. Angeli. Italian
King Richard III
  Richard the Third, a tragedy
Locrine [spurious and doubtful work], see Locrine
Much ado about nothing
  The comedy of Much ado about nothing
Raigne of King Edvvard the Third, see Edward III
    (Drama)
Richard III, see his King Richard III
Songs, see the file of Poetical works preceding.
Sonnets
  Shak-speares Sonnets   1609 (repr. 1926)
  Sonnets, and A lover's complaint   Alden
  The original order of
    Shakespeare's sonnets   Bray
  Shakespeare's sonnets   Brooke
  The sonnets   Mosher, publ.
Sonnets (Translations)
  Le secret de Shakespeare;
    les sonnets   French. L'Hommedé
  Shakespeare sonnets   German. George. 1909
  Sonnette   German. George. 1931
  Sonetos   Spanish. Astrana Marín
Sonnets (Criticism)
  Godwin. A new study of the sonnets
  Hitchcock. Remarks on the Sonnets
Taming of the shrew
  A modern prompt book of...Taming of
    the shrew.   Bacon and Kennedy
  The taming of the shrew. Coriolanus. Booklovers ed.
  Catharine and Petruchio   Garrick
  The taming of the shrew, a comic
    opera by Goetz.
  [a secondary entry with main entry under Goetz]
  Shakespeare's comedy of the Taming
    of the shrew.   Rolfe
Taming of the shrew. (Translations)
  Kunst über alle künste   German. Kohler
  Der widerpenstigen zähmung   German. Weber
Two noble kinsmen, see Fletcher, John. The two noble
    kinsmen.
Venus and Adonis
  Adaptation of Shakespeare's poem Venus and Adonis
The winter's tale
  The comedy of the winter's tale; abr. by Hiestand
  Shakespeare's The winter's tale; ed. by Hudson

```
SHAKESPEARE.  Works about
   SHAKESPEARE  —  ADAPTATIONS
   SHAKESPEARE  —  AUTHORSHIP
   SHAKESPEARE  —  BIBLIOGRAPHY
   SHAKESPEARE  —  COMEDIES
   SHAKESPEARE  —  CONCORDANCES, INDEXES, ETC.
            etc., etc.
```

For a simplified arrangement of Shakespeare according to Rule 25, *see* the Comprehensive example, Appendix V.

b) Arrangement 2 (For large reference collections) [23]

Arrange entries in the following main groups:—1. Complete works, 2. Selected works: Partial collections (miscellaneous), 3. Selected works: Particular groups, 4. Single works, 5. Spurious and doubtful works, 6. Selections: anthologies, extracts, quotations, etc., 7. Subject entries.

(1) Complete works

Arrange in the following order:—

(a) Manuscripts and facsimiles of manuscripts

Arrange by date. A facsimile is arranged by date of the original.

(b) Texts in the original language

Arrange first by date and then by editor, disregarding variations in the wording of the title. Supply approximate date. Facsimiles and reprints are arranged first by date of the original and secondarily by date of the reprint.

(c) Translations

Arrange alphabetically by language and under language subarrange by date.

(d) Criticisms of a particular edition or translation

Arrange immediately following the text of that edition or translation.

(2) Selected works: partial collections

Arrange like Complete works

(3) Selected works: particular groups

Arrange alphabetically by the best-known group-title in the original language, and under each group-title arrange the entries like Complete works.

Note: If this separate arrangement of special groups is not desired, the groups may be included either with the other partial collections (2) or with the Single works (4).

---

[23] Since any general scheme has to be adapted to the individual author, no examples are given under Rules 26: b and 26: c.

(4) Single works

Arrange alphabetically by the best known title in the original language (cf. 26: *a*3). Under each title subarrange as follows: —

(a) Texts in the original language. Arrange like Complete works.

(b) Translations. Arrange as under Complete works.

(c) Criticisms, etc. Arrange alphabetically by author of the criticism. *Exception:* a criticism of a particular edition or translation files immediately after that edition or translation.

(5) Spurious and doubtful works

Arrange (*a*) Collections; (*b*) Single titles. Under each subarrange like Complete works.

(6) Selections: anthologies, etc.

Arrange like Complete works. If preferred, the subarrangement under original texts and translations may be by title.

(7) Subject entries

See Rule 25: *b*

c) Arrangement 3 (ALTERNATIVE rule for large collections)

The distinguishing characteristic of this alternative arrangement is that translations and criticisms form separate groups following the entire body of original texts.

Arrange the entries in the following main groups: —1. Original texts, 2. Translations, 3. Biography and general criticism, 4. Criticism of individual works, 5. Other subject entries

(1) Original texts

Arrange as follows: —

(a) Complete works

(b) Selected works

(c) Single works

(d) Spurious and doubtful works

(e) Selections

Subarrange each section as in 26: *b* 1-6, omitting translations and criticisms.

(2) Translations

Arrange by language and under language subarrange according to the sections *a-e* under Original texts.

Note: English translations may be placed first, if preferred.

    (3) Biography and general criticism
        Arrange by main entry.

    (4) Criticism of single works
        Arrange by the title of the Single work and subarrange
    by the author of the criticism.

    (5) Other subject entries
        See Rule 25: *b*

27. Corporate entries (Institutions, organizations, societies, etc.)

For corporate entries under country, state, city, etc., *see* Place arrangement (Rules 31-32) and example under U.S. Congress (Rule 38: *c*).

a) Under the corporate author headings for institutions, societies, etc. (e.g., churches, denominations, museums, universities, etc.) arrange titles and added entries according to the rules adopted for personal author entries (Rule 25).

b) Arrange subdivisions, both author and subject, in one alphabet.

```
Baptists.   Alabama
Baptists.   Alabama.  State convention
BAPTISTS.   BIOGRAPHY
Baptists.   Board of education
BAPTISTS.   HISTORY
Baptists.   Massachusetts.  Berkshire association
BAPTISTS.   OREGON
Baptists.   Oregon.  General association
BAPTISTS.   U.S.

Catholic church
CATHOLIC CHURCH
CATHOLIC CHURCH.  BIBLIOGRAPHY
Catholic church.  Catechisms
CATHOLIC CHURCH.  CATECHISMS AND CREEDS
Catholic church.  Councils
CATHOLIC CHURCH.  DISCIPLINE
CATHOLIC CHURCH.  HISTORY
Catholic church.  Liturgy and ritual
CATHOLIC CHURCH.  LITURGY AND RITUAL
Catholic church.  Pope
Catholic church.  Treaties

Harvard university
HARVARD UNIVERSITY
Harvard university.  Arnold arboretum
HARVARD UNIVERSITY.  BIOGRAPHY
Harvard university.  Class of 1883
Harvard university.  Class of 1901
Harvard university.  Dental school
Harvard university.  Dramatic club
HARVARD UNIVERSITY.  EXAMINATIONS
```

Harvard university. Harvard alumni association
Harvard university. Library
HARVARD UNIVERSITY. LIBRARY

When a large number of entries exist under a corporate heading, a special scheme of arrangement may become advisable. Author and subject entries may be separated; and/or geographical subdivisions may be formed into a separate group. The Library of Congress indicates by the use of bold-faced type that, under a university, entries for alumni, student and similar organizations (e.g., Harvard university, Class of 1901, Harvard university, Dramatic club) may be filed separately. Such variations from a single alphabet should be made by large libraries as the need for them arises.

28.-30. ANONYMOUS CLASSICS: BIBLE AND OTHER SACRED BOOKS

Variation of cataloging practice in the formation of Bible and other anonymous classic headings makes it difficult to formulate a generally acceptable filing arrangement. The Library of Congress is revising its Bible headings to give language division precedence over form division in main-entry headings, e.g., Bible. *English. Selections* instead of Bible. *Selections. English;* and by using the latter as an added entry, makes possible a double arrangement. *See* Conspectus of L.C. Bible arrangement, Appendix IV. Since few libraries require this elaborate system of double entries and double arrangements, the following schemes are recommended: —

Rule 28 is an arrangement, based on the Library of Congress revised headings, that is *suitable for large collections.*

Rule 29 is a simplified, more nearly alphabetic arrangement, *suitable for smaller and medium sized collections.*

For a strictly alphabetical arrangement for small collections, see Appendix V.

28. Bible. For large collections, based on Library of Congress revised headings.

Arrange Bible entries in groups in the following order: —

a) Bible. Manuscripts
Arrange by language and under each language by parts. Refer from the parts, viz., Bible. O.T. Manuscripts, *see* Bible. Manuscripts. Language. O.T.

b) Bible as a whole
(1) Texts: arrange alphabetically by language. A polyglot Bible may file before the single languages or in its alphabetical place.
Under each language, subarrange in two main groups: —

(a) By date, and then by version or editor.

ALTERNATIVE: Libraries that prefer to keep versions together may do so by arranging first by version or editor and then by date; entries with date only preceding those arranged by version, viz.,

```
Bible.  English.  1811
        English.  Authorized.  1611
        English.  Authorized.  1763
        English.  Douai.  1852
        English.  Fenton.  1938
        English.  Geneva.  1590
        English.  Moffatt.  1926
        English.  Moffatt.  1935
```

(b) By form division, alphabetically, as

```
Bible.  Language.  Lessons, Liturgical
Bible.  Language.  Paraphrases
Bible.  Language.  Selections
```

Under the form divisions, the further subarrangement may be either by date (Library of Congress) or by title; the latter of these is to be preferred by public libraries because the titles are usually distinctive.

(2) Bible as subject

Arrange alphabetically by subject subdivision, and under each subdivision by main entry.

c) Bible. Old Testament.

(1) Texts: arrange as in b 1 above.

(2) Subject: arrange as in b 2 above.

(3) Parts; under each part arrange by language and by subject as above. The parts of the Old and New Testaments may be arranged either in alphabetical or in canonical order. The alphabetical is recommended since the canonical is no longer familiarly known. If the canonical is used, the parts should be listed on a guide-card at the front of each drawer, or a numbered alphabetical index should be filed at the beginning of the section, see Index table, Appendix IV. Groups of books, such as the Pentateuch, should file in their alphabetical places; or, if the canonical order is adopted, before the first book of the group.

d) Bible. New Testament

Arrange like the Old Testament

e) Bible (titles, etc.)

Bible. Manuscripts
   Bible. Manuscripts, Church Slavic. N.T. Gospels
   Bible. Manuscripts, Gothic. Codex argenteus
   Bible. Manuscripts, Greek. Codex vaticanus
   BIBLE. MANUSCRIPTS, GREEK. CODEX VATICANUS
   Bible. Manuscripts, Greek. O.T. Genesis
   Bible. Manuscripts, Greek. N.T. Codex vaticanus
   Bible. Manuscripts, Latin. O.T. Psalms
   BIBLE. MANUSCRIPTS
   Bible. Manuscripts. Facsimiles

Bible. Texts, arranged by language
   Bible. Polyglot. 1901
   Bible. Armenian
   Bible. English. 1881. Revised
   Bible. English. 1911. Authorized
   Bible. English. 1922. Moffatt
   Bible. English. 1931. Authorized
   Bible. English. Paraphrases. 1902
     The Christ of the ages in words of Holy writ.
   Bible. English. Paraphrases. 1934
     The Bible in song.
   Bible. English. Selections. 1887
     Commands and promises for daily meditations.
   Bible. English. Selections. 1911
     The busy man's Bible.
   Bible. English. Selections. 1915
     Gems from the Bible.
   Bible. English. Selections. 1918-21
     The shorter Bible.
   Bible. English. Selections. 1929
     Familiar Bible quotations.
   Bible. French. 1856. Martin
   Bible. French. 1858. Martin
   Bible. French. Selections
   Bible. German. 1580. Luther
   Bible. German. 1865. Allioli
   Bible. German. Paraphrases
   Bible. Portuguese

BIBLE. SUBJECT
   BIBLE — BIBLIOGRAPHY
   BIBLE — COMMENTARIES
   BIBLE — HISTORY
   BIBLE — HISTORY OF BIBLICAL EVENTS
   BIBLE — INTRODUCTIONS

Bible. Old Testament. Texts
   Bible. O.T. Manuscripts
     see Bible. Manuscripts
   Bible. O.T. English. 1917
   Bible. O.T. English. 1920
   Bible. O.T. English. Selections. 1904
     Narratives of the beginnings of Hebrew history.

```
        Bible.  O.T.  English.  Selections.  1906
            Bible stories (Old Testament)
        Bible.  O.T.  German.  1914
        Bible.  O.T.  Hebrew.  1667

    BIBLE.  O.T.  SUBJECT
        BIBLE.  O.T.  — ANTIQUITIES
        BIBLE.  O.T.  — BIOGRAPHY
        BIBLE.  O.T.  — COMMENTARIES

    Bible.  O.T.  Parts
        Bible.  O.T.  Amos.  English.  1911
        Bible.  O.T.  Amos.  English.  1929
        Bible.  O.T.  Amos.  French.  1913
        BIBLE.  O.T.  AMOS
        Bible.  O.T.  Apocrypha.  English.  1888
        BIBLE.  O.T.  APOCRYPHA
        Bible.  O.T.  Apocrypha.  Baruch
        Bible.  O.T.  Apocrypha.  Esdras
        Bible.  O.T.  Apocrypha.  Maccabees
        Bible.  O.T.  APOCRYPHA.  MACCABEES
        Bible.  O.T.  Apocrypha.  1 Maccabees
        Bible.  O.T.  Apocrypha.  2 Maccabees
        Bible.  O.T.  Apocryphal books
        Bible.  O.T.  Chronicles.  English
        Bible.  O.T.  Chronicles.  Latin
        BIBLE.  O.T.  CHRONICLES.
        Bible.  O.T.  1 Chronicles
        Bible.  O.T.  2 Chronicles
        Bible.  O.T.  Daniel
        Bible.  O.T.  Deuteronomy
        Bible.  O.T.  Genesis
        Bible.  O.T.  Heptateuch
        Bible.  O.T.  Maccabees
            see  Bible.  O.T.  Apocrypha.  Maccabees
        Bible.  O.T.  Pentateuch
        Bible.  O.T.  Samuel

    Bible.  New Testament
        Arrange like O.T.

    Bible.  Titles, etc.
        Bible and science
        Bible in Spain
        Bible plays
```

29. Bible. Alphabetic order for smaller collections

This is a simplified scheme for libraries that prefer an alphabetic order under the Bible and its parts. The English language may be omitted, if preferred, in order to bring the English texts first. Language divisions have been dropped under subordinate parts of the Old and New Testaments, because the libraries using this scheme will probably not have enough texts under any one part to make language division necessary.

a) Bible as a whole

Arrange all divisions (language, form and subject) in one alphabet.

Under each language, subarrange texts by date and then, if needed, by version or editor. (Cf. Alternative under Rule 28: *b* 1 *a*)

When the same heading is used for a text and for a subject entry, the text precedes the subject.

b) Bible. Old Testament

Arrange all divisions, including the parts, in one alphabet; subarranging texts as above.

c) Bible. New Testament

Arrange like Old Testament.

d) Bible. Titles, etc.

```
Bible
    Bible. 1881. Revised
    Bible. 1911. Authorized
    Bible. 1922. Moffatt
    Bible. 1931. Authorized24
    BIBLE
    BIBLE — ANTIQUITIES
    Bible. Armenian
    BIBLE — BIBLIOGRAPHY
    BIBLE — COMMENTARIES
    Bible. Dutch
    Bible. French
    BIBLE. MANUSCRIPTS
    Bible. Manuscripts. Facsimiles
    Bible. Manuscripts, Greek. Codex vaticanus
    Bible. Manuscripts, Greek. O.T. Genesis
    Bible. Manuscripts, Greek. N.T.
    Bible. Manuscripts, Latin. O.T. Psalms
    Bible. Manx
    Bible. Paraphrases
        The Bible in song
        The Christ of the ages in words of Holy writ
        Neue Bibel...nachgedichtet von Kaegi
        Récits sacrés
    Bible. Polyglot
    BIBLE — PROPHECIES
    Bible. Selections
        Die Bibel in auswahl für haus
        The busy man's Bible
        Familiar Bible quotations
        Perlen der Bibel
        The shorter Bible
```

---

[24] If "English" is inserted in the heading, these first four entries will file after Bible. Dutch.

```
      BIBLE - STUDY
      Bible.  Swedish
      BIBLE - VERSIONS
   Bible.  Old Testament
      Bible.  O.T.  1917
      Bible.  O.T.  1920
      BIBLE.  O.T.
      Bible.  O.T.  Amos
      BIBLE.  O.T.  AMOS
      BIBLE.  O.T. - ANTIQUITIES
      Bible.  O.T.  Apocalypse of Baruch
         see  Bible.  O.T. Apocryphal books.  Apocalypse of
               Baruch
      Bible.  O.T.  Apocrypha
      BIBLE.  O.T.  APOCRYPHA
      Bible.  O.T.  Apocrypha.  Baruch
      Bible.  O.T.  Apocrypha.  Esdras
      BIBLE.  O.T. - BIOGRAPHY
      Bible.  O.T.  Baruch
         see  Bible.  O.T. Apocrypha. Baruch
      Bible.  O.T.  Baruch, Apocalypse of
         see  Bible.  O.T. Apocryphal books.  Apocalypse of
               Baruch
      Bible.  O.T.  Chronicles
      BIBLE.  O.T.  CHRONICLES
      Bible.  O.T.  I Chronicles
      Bible.  O.T.  II Chronicles
      BIBLE.  O.T. - COMMENTARIES
      Bible.  O.T.  German
      BIBLE.  O.T. - HISTORY
      Bible.  O.T.  Italian
      Bible.  O.T.  Manuscripts
         see  Bible.  Manuscripts
      Bible.  O.T.  Paraphrases
      Bible.  O.T.  Pentateuch
      Bible.  O.T.  Psalms
      Bible.  O.T.  Psalms I-XX
      Bible.  O.T.  Psalms XXIII
      Bible.  O.T.  Psalms.  Paraphrases
      Bible.  O.T.  Selections
   Bible.  New Testament
         Arrange like Old Testament
   Bible.  Titles, etc.
      BIBLE AND SCIENCE
      The Bible and the child
      BIBLE IN LITERATURE
      Bible in Spain
      Bible plays
      Bible student's companion
```

Note: The smaller public libraries may prefer to interfile *all* entries beginning with the word Bible in one straight alphabet. *See* Bible in the Comprehensive example, Appendix V.

30. Other anonymous classics and sacred books

a) Follow the same principles as for the arrangement of Bible entries.

An alphabetic interfiling of form and subject subdivisions is suggested unless the collection of entries is large.

```
Talmud  [texts]
TALMUD
Talmud. Appendices
TALMUD. BIBLIOGRAPHY
Talmud. Manuscripts
Talmud. Selections. English
Talmud. Selections. German
Talmud. Barakoth
Talmud. Megillah          ·   or  interfile the parts with
TALMUD. MEGILLAH                  the other subdivisions,
Talmud. Nashim                    if preferred.
Talmud. Nashim. English
Talmud Yerushalmi
```

b) When the name of an historical person is used in the heading of an anonymous classic, e.g., Charlemagne (Romances, etc.), the entry for the real person should precede the anonymous classic entries.

```
Charlemagne,  742-814
CHARLEMAGNE,  742-814
CHARLEMAGNE — CANONIZATION
CHARLEMAGNE — DRAMA
Charlemagne and his knights
Charlemagne (Drama)
Charlemagne.  Gesta Karoli Magni ad Carcassonam et
      Narbonam
Charlemagne (Romances, etc)
Charlemagne.  Vita Karoli Magni sec. XII
Charlemagne.  Voyage à Jérusalem et à Constantinople
Charlemagne.  Ystoria de Carolo Magno
```

31.-32. PLACE ARRANGEMENT

Preliminary note. Entries beginning with the same geographical name may be analyzed into the following types: —

1. A place (city, state, country, etc.) as a corporate author. This includes the entries for works by the government of the place and by its official divisions, i.e., bureaus, departments, offices, commissions, committees, the army, the navy; also the entries for the texts of charters, constitutions, laws and statutes, ordinances and treaties. And the subject entries for the same.

2. The local institutions (churches, libraries, museums, schools, universities, etc.) that are entered under the name of the place. Both author and subject entries.
3. A place as subject, with the subject subdivisions.
4. Other places of the same name (e.g., London; London, Ohio; London, Ont.) each of which may have entries as listed in 1-3 above.
5. Societies and other organizations whose names begin with the place name (e.g., London mathematical society); both author and subject entries. These are not necessarily located in the place.
6. Geographical, ecclesiastical, and other headings beginning with the same name, such as counties, townships, rivers, lakes, gulfs, mountains, etc.; e.g., New York (City), New York (Colony), New York (County), New York (State), London (Diocese), Los Angeles river, Washington County.
7. Inverted headings, such as Concord, Battle of, Berlin, Treaty of, Washington, Fort. Some of the inverted headings are also geographical headings, e.g., Washington, Mt., Mexico, Gulf of.
8. Names of ships, etc., e.g., Pennsylvania (Battleship), Los Angeles (Airship).
9. Titles and phrase subject headings beginning with the same name.

The problem is to combine these various types into one or more groups so that users of the catalog may locate a specific entry with a minimum of searching, and yet to have due regard to the needs of research workers. There has been no uniform library practice in the arrangement of place entries. *Two orders of arrangement* have therefore been selected for recommendation. *Rule 31 gives a grouped order,* either a three-group or a two-group arrangement; and *Rule 32 gives* a single group or *straight alphabetic arrangement.*

31. Place arrangement (Grouped order)

a) Three-group order
Arrange entries beginning with the same geographical term in three main groups, as follows: —1. Place as corporate author with subject entries about the corporate author, 2. Place as subject, 3. Societies, organizations, titles, and all other entries beginning with the same geographical name.

Note: The chief advantage of the three-group order is that it concentrates the official and nonofficial author entries in one alphabet and so facilitates the checking of bibliographical lists and references. To libraries in which the segregation of the corporate author entries is not of paramount importance, the two-group order (*see* alternative Rule 31:*b*) is recommended. The latter arrangement has the advantage of keeping in the same group the subject entries for a place as corporate author and the general subject entries for the place and thus eliminates many cross references.

(1) Place as corporate author (cf. Preliminary note 1-2)

Interfile in one alphabet the entries, both author and subject for the official divisions and for the nonofficial local institutions.

Note: The Library of Congress on its printed cards distinguishes by the use of italics in the subhead, entries for official divisions from entries for nonofficial local institutions, e.g., Washington, D.C. *Board of health* (official) and Washington, D.C. Board of trade (nonofficial) and files them in separate groups. A few of the larger libraries may prefer to follow the Library of Congress practice; but in general this is not recommended because users of the catalog do not distinguish between official and nonofficial headings. For those libraries that prefer to file nonofficial public institutions in the third group with societies and other organizations, an example will be found under New York (Appendix I).

(a) Arrange headings consisting of the place name followed by such terms as *defendant, plaintiff,* etc., before any of the official divisions.

(b) Arrange headings of the official bureaus, departments, etc., and of local institutions by the *first* word of the subhead, e.g.,

```
U.S. - Bureau of education
U.S. - Dept. of agriculture
```

with reference from the distinctive subject word in the subhead, e.g.,

```
U.S. - Education, Bureau of  see
U.S. - Bureau of education
```

(c) ALTERNATIVE: Disregard the words Board of, Bureau of, Dept. of, etc., and alphabet by the *topical* word or phrase in the subhead. Underline the topical word and make a blanket reference from the disregarded phrase.

Note: The advantages of this alternative are: that a person may remember the topical word but may not know whether the object of his search is a bureau, a board or a department; that in case of reorganization and change of name, the distinctive part of the name is likely to be retained; that there is a subject value in arrangement by topical word.

The objection to this arrangement is that there is no standard practice in regard to the adoption of the topical word. Some libraries disregard the topical order when the official name begins with an adjective, such as Advisory, Central, Federal, National, etc., and alphabet by these; other libraries do not. If the topical word order is followed in all cases, cross references should be made from the official name beginning with an adjective.

```
U.S.   Advisory council on social security,  see
          U.S.   Advisory council on social security
U.S.   Bureau of agricultural economics
U.S.   Dept. of agriculture
U.S.   Federal committee on apprenticeship
U.S.   Bureau of...
       Government bureaus are arranged by the topical
       word or phrase underlined in the name, e.g.,
       U.S. - Bureau of education
U.S.   Bureau of the census
U.S.   Census office
U.S.   Dept. of commerce
U.S.   Council of national defense,  see  U.S.
          Council of national defense
U.S.   Bureau of education
U.S.   Office of education
U.S.   Federal committee on apprenticeship,  see
          U.S.   Federal committee on apprenticeship
U.S.   Bureau of foreign and domestic commerce
U.S.   Commission on industrial relations
U.S.   National bureau of standards,  see  U.S.
          National bureau of standards
U.S.   Council of national defense
U.S.   Advisory council on social security
U.S.   National bureau of standards
```

(d) When there are author and subject entries for the same heading, file the subject after the author.

(2) Place as subject (cf. Preliminary note 3)
Arrange the subject subdivisions alphabetically. (cf. *Arrangement under Subject,* Rules 33-35 and *Chronological arrangement,* Rule 38)

(3) Societies, organizations, titles and all other entries beginning with the same geographical name (cf. Preliminary note 5-9)
Arrange alphabetically by the word, or words, following the place name, disregarding punctuation.

(4) When there are two or more places of the same name, the places are arranged alphabetically by the designation following the name, e.g.

```
London            New York (City)
London, Ohio      New York (Colony)
London, Ontario   New York (County)
                  New York (State)                      .
```

Author and subject entries are arranged under each place, as in a.-b., but entries for societies, organizations, etc., *without country, state, or other designation after the place name,* file in a final group (3. above) after the entries for the separate places.

```
London  (corporate author and subject entries about
     corporate author)
  London
  London.  Aëronautical exhibition, 1868
  London.  Charing Cross hospital
  London.  Corporation
  London.  County council
  LONDON.  COUNTY COUNCIL
  London.  National gallery
  LONDON.  NATIONAL GALLERY
  London.  Ordinances
  LONDON.  ST. PAUL'S CATHEDRAL
  London.  School board
  London.  Stationers' company
  London.  Stock exchange
  LONDON.  STOCK EXCHANGE
  London.  University
  LONDON.  UNIVERSITY
LONDON  (subject entries about place)
  LONDON — ANTIQUITIES                          .
  LONDON — COUNTY COUNCIL
       For material on this subject,  see
       the preceding file.
  LONDON — DESCRIPTION
  LONDON — HISTORY
  LONDON — SOCIAL LIFE AND CUSTOMS
  LONDON — STOCK EXCHANGE
       For material on this subject, see
       the preceding file.
  LONDON — WATER SUPPLY

London (Diocese)
London, Ohio
London, Ont.
  London, Ont.  Council
  London, Ont.  University of western Ontario
  LONDON, ONT.
  LONDON, ONT. — ANTIQUITIES
London (titles, etc.)
  London; a guide...
  London and Londoners
  London and Middlesex archaeological society
```

London and Middlesex historical society, London, Ont.
London magazine
London Shakespeare league
London. University
    For material by or about this institution,
    see Author file preceding.

Washington, D.C. (Corporate author and subject entries
        about corporate author)
    Washington, D.C. Academy of sciences
        See Washington academy of sciences
        in the file of Titles, etc. following.
    Washington, D.C. All souls church
    Washington, D.C. Board of health
    Washington, D.C. Board of trade
    Washington, D.C. Conference on the limitation
        of armaments, 1921-1922
    Washington, D.C. Council
    Washington, D.C. Council of social agencies
    Washington, D.C. National gallery
    Washington, D.C. Public library
    WASHINGTON, D.C. PUBLIC LIBRARY
    Washington, D.C. Water dept.
    WASHINGTON, D.C. WHITE HOUSE
    WASHINGTON, D.C. (Subject entries about place)
    WASHINGTON, D.C. — DESCRIPTION
    WASHINGTON, D.C. — HISTORY
    WASHINGTON, D.C. — WATER SUPPLY
Washington (State) (Corporate author and subject
        entries about corporate author)
    Washington (State) Agricultural experiment station,
        Pullman
    Washington (State) Bureau of labor
    Washington (State) Canal commission
    Washington (State) Geological survey
    WASHINGTON (STATE) GEOLOGICAL SURVEY
    Washington (State) State college, Pullman
    Washington (State) State forestry board
    Washington (State) State historical society, Tacoma
        See Washington state historical society, Tacoma,
        Wash. in the file of Titles, etc. following.
    Washington (State) State library, Olympia
    Washington (State) University
    WASHINGTON (STATE) (Subject entries about place)
    WASHINGTON (STATE) — DESCRIPTION AND TRAVEL
    WASHINGTON (STATE) — HISTORY
    WASHINGTON (STATE) — SOCIAL LIFE AND CUSTOMS
Washington (Ter.)
    Washington (Ter.) Auditor's Office
    Washington (Ter.) Laws, statutes, etc.
    WASHINGTON (TER.) — HISTORY
Washington (Titles, etc.)
    Washington; a poem

```
    Washington academy of sciences
    WASHINGTON (BATTLESHIP)
    Washington Co., Ala.
    Washington county historical society, Abingdon, Va.
    WASHINGTON, FORT
    WASHINGTON, MT.
    Washington state bar association
    Washington state historical society, Tacoma, Wash.
    Washington university, St. Louis
```

See also the examples shown under New York and United States in Appendix I.

b) Two-group order

Follow the general directions under Rule 31*a*, but interfile in one group the author and subject entries.

```
London  (place)
    London
    LONDON
    London.  Aëronautical exhibition, 1868
    LONDON — ANTIQUITIES
    London.  Charing Cross hospital
    London.  County council
    LONDON.  COUNTY COUNCIL
    LONDON — DESCRIPTION
    London.  Guildhall library
    LONDON — HISTORY
    London.  National gallery
    LONDON.  NATIONAL GALLERY
    London.  Naval conference, 1930
    London.  Ordinances
    London.  St Paul's cathedral
    London.  School board
    LONDON — SOCIAL LIFE AND CUSTOMS
    London.  University
    London (Diocese)
    London, Ohio
    London, Ont.
    LONDON, ONT. — ANTIQUITIES
    London, Ont.  Council
    London, Ont.  University of western Ontario
London  (Titles, etc.)
    London; a guide...
    London and Londoners
    London and Middlesex archaeological society

Washington, D.C.
    Washington, D.C.  Academy of sciences
        see  Washington academy of sciences in the
        file of Titles, etc., following
    Washington, D.C.  All souls church
    Washington, D.C.  Board of health
    Washington, D.C.  Board of trade
```

```
Washington, D.C.  Conference on limitation
    of armaments, 1921-1922
Washington, D.C.  Council
Washington, D.C.  Council of social agencies
WASHINGTON, D.C. - HISTORY
Washington, D.C.  National gallery
Washington, D.C.  Public library
WASHINGTON, D.C. - PUBLIC LIBRARY
WASHINGTON, D.C. - STREETS
Washington, D.C.  Water Dept.
WASHINGTON, D.C.  WATER SUPPLY
WASHINGTON, D.C.  WHITE HOUSE
Washington (state)
Washington (state)  Agricultural experiment station,
    Pullman
Washington (state)  Bureau of labor
Washington (state)  Canal commission
WASHINGTON (STATE)  DESCRIPTION AND TRAVEL
Washington (state)  Geological survey
WASHINGTON (STATE)  HISTORY
Washington (state)  State college, Pullman
Washington (state)  State forestry board
Washington (state)  State historical society, Tacoma
    see  Washington state historical society, Tacoma,
    Wash. in file of Titles, etc., following
Washington (state)  State library, Olympia
Washington (state)  University
Washington (Ter.)
Washington (Ter.)  Auditor's office
WASHINGTON (TER.) - HISTORY
Washington (Ter.)  Laws, statutes, etc.
Washington  (Titles, etc.)
Washington; a poem
Washington academy of sciences
WASHINGTON (BATTLESHIP)
Washington Co., Ala.
Washington county historical society, Abingdon, Va.
WASHINGTON, FORT
WASHINGTON, MT.
Washington state bar association
Washington state historical society, Tacoma, Wash.
Washington university, St. Louis
```

32. Place arrangement (Alphabetic order)

a) File entries beginning with the same geographical name in one alphabet, arranging by the word following the name, disregarding both punctuation and typography.

b) Subject entries are filed immediately after the author entries of the same heading.

c) In the rare instances when a title heading is identical with a subject heading, arrange alphabetically by the main entry.

d) Two or more places of the same name are alphabeted by the distinguishing designation following the name.

Note: Library of Congress omits country or state designation after the names of chief cities; but in order to keep the author and subject entries for a chief city from being scattered throughout the alphabet under the place name, it is necessary to insert the country or state designation.

```
Concord  [a poem]
Concord and Lexington
Concord antiquarian society, Concord, Mass.
CONCORD, BATTLE OF
Concord days
Concord library corporation, Concordsville, Pa.
Concord, Me.
CONCORD, ME.
Concord, Mass.
CONCORD, MASS.
Concord, Mass.  Convention, July 14, 1774
CONCORD, MASS. — DIRECTORIES
CONCORD, MASS. — HISTORY
Concord, Mass.  Trinity church
Concord, N.H.
CONCORD, N.H.
Concord, N.H.  City history commission
Concord, N.H.  Ordinances
Concord, N.H.  Public library
Concord railroad corporation
CONCORD RIVER
CONCORD SCHOOL OF PHILOSOPHY
Concord, Tenn.  Farragut school

Washington academy of science
Washington and Lee university
Washington council of social agencies
Washington county, Ohio
Washington, D.C.
WASHINGTON, D.C.
Washington, D.C.  Chamber of commerce
Washington, D.C.  Conference on the limitation of
    armaments, 1921-1922
WASHINGTON, D.C. — DESCRIPTION
Washington, D.C.  National gallery of art
WASHINGTON, D.C. — SOCIAL LIFE AND CUSTOMS
WASHINGTON, D.C.  WHITE HOUSE
The Washington enterprise
Washington humane society, Washington, D.C.
Washington merry-go-round
Washington, Mt.
Washington (State)
WASHINGTON (STATE)
Washington (State)  Bureau of labor
```

```
Washington (State)  Canal commission
Washington (State)  Constitution
Washington (State)  Dept. of agriculture
WASHINGTON (STATE) – DESCRIPTION AND TRAVEL
Washington (State)  Geological survey
Washington state historical society, Tacoma, Wash.
Washington (State)  Laws, statutes, etc.
WASHINGTON (STATE) – SOCIAL LIFE AND CUSTOMS
Washington (State)  State college, Pullman
Washington (State)  State library, Olympia
Washington (State)  University
Washington surveying and rating bureau, Seattle
Washington (Ter.)  Auditor's office
Washington (Ter.)  Governor
Washington university, St. Louis
Washington wool growers' association
```

See also the examples shown under New York and United States in Appendix I.

33.-35. SUBJECT ARRANGEMENT

Preliminary note: Analysis of the Library of Congress list of subject headings[25] shows that the following types of heading may have to be considered in subject arrangement: —

1. The subject without subdivision.
2. Subject with form or subject divisions, e.g., ART—EXHIBITIONS, ART—PERIODICALS.
3. Subject with period divisions, e.g., ENGLISH LITERATURE—17TH CENTURY, FRANCE—HISTORY—REVOLUTION.
4. Subject with geographical divisions, e.g., ART—ITALY.
5. Inverted subject heading: (a) subject followed by an adjective form, e.g., ART, ANCIENT; ART, ITALIAN; ART, MUNICIPAL; and (b) subject followed by an inverted phrase, e.g., BIRDS, PROTECTION OF.
6. Subject followed by a term in parentheses. Such subjects may be of more than one kind, i.e.:

   a. The parenthetical term limits the subject to a particular field or aspect, e.g., ANALYSIS (CHEMISTRY), ANALYSIS (MATHEMATICS), BANKRUPTCY (INTERNATIONAL LAW). The majority of parenthetical term subjects are of this kind and frequently are *See* references.

   b. The parenthetical term indicates a distinctly different subject, one belonging to another field of knowledge, e.g., AUTHORS (GAME), BIOGRAPHY (AS A LITERARY FORM), CALCULUS (PATHOLOGY), WASHINGTON (SHIP).

[25] Library of Congress, *Subject headings*, 3rd ed. Washington: Govt. print. off., 1928).

c. The parenthetical term may be used merely to indicate a separate grouping, e.g., ENGLISH LITERATURE (COLLECTIONS).

Note: The Library of Congress regards the parenthesis as a highly useful, flexible form, the use of which may be extended in future. Its extended use will probably be needed only in very large libraries or in specialized catalogs. Most libraries do not require the third kind of parenthetical subject. For instance, ENGLISH LITERATURE—COLLECTIONS as a form heading belonging to group 2 above, is generally to be preferred to ENGLISH LITERATURE (COLLECTIONS)

7. Phrase headings beginning with the subject word, e.g., ART AND STATE.

8. Few, if any, subjects present all of the above types; but particular subjects may have also a special subdivision, e.g., ENGLISH LITERATURE—CATHOLIC AUTHORS, ENGLISH LITERATURE—IRISH AUTHORS.

Rule 33 gives the general alphabetic arrangement of entries under a subject heading.

It is possible to arrange the subdivisions of a subject in a varying number of groups, depending upon the size of the catalog and the requirements of the library. Two arrangements have been selected for recommendation: *Rule 34 illustrates order of groups as shown in Library of Congress list. Rule 35 gives an alternative arrangement for libraries that prefer fewer groups and a more nearly alphabetic order.*

33. Subject arrangement

Arrange entries of the same subject heading alphabetically by the main entry of the book; or, if the entry is a subject analytic by an author other than the author of the book, arrange by the author of the analytic.

```
ENGLISH POETRY – COLLECTIONS

A book of English love songs

Cody, Sherwin,   ed.
    A selection from the great English poets

An English garner

Noyes, Alfred,   ed.
    A poet's anthology of poems


ROMANTICISM

Babbitt, Irving
    Romantic melancholy, (In Foerster, Norman,   ed.
       American critical essays, xixth and xxth centuries.)

Beers, H. A.
    History of English romanticism in the eighteenth
century
```

Boyesen, H. H.
    Essays on German literature
        Contents: Goethe, Schiller. The <u>romantic</u>
        <u>school</u> <u>in</u> <u>Germany</u>
Cory, H. H.
    Spenser, Thomson and romanticism. (<u>In</u> Modern
        language association. Publications)

34. Subject arrangement 1 (Based on the L.C. list)

a) Arrange a subject and its subheads, etc., in the following order: —

(1) Subject without division. Subarrange by main entry (cf. Rule 33).

(2) Form and subject divisions. Arrange alphabetically by division.

(3) Period divisions. Arrange chronologically.

Phrase period divisions, e.g., U.S.—HISTORY—REVOLUTION, U.S.—HISTORY—CIVIL WAR are arranged chronologically and not alphabetically. Inclusive periods file before subordinate periods.

Under LANGUAGE AND LITERATURE subjects, such subheads as FRENCH LANGUAGE—OLD FRENCH, GERMAN LITERATURE—EARLY MODERN (TO 1700) are regarded as period divisions.

The divisions ANCIENT, MEDIEVAL, RENAISSANCE and MODERN are treated as adjectival inversions and not as period divisions, except when used as a subdivision under HISTORY, and are filed in group 6 below.

(4) Special divisions. (*See* Preliminary note 8) Arrange alphabetically.

(5) Geographical divisions. Arrange alphabetically.

Inverted subject headings formed with a racial or linguistic adjective, e.g., ART, AMERICAN (ENGLISH, ITALIAN, etc.) are not regarded as geographical divisions, but are included in group 7 below.

(6) Subject followed by a parenthetical term denoting *limitation* (cf. Prelim. note 6a). Arrange, if more than one, alphabetically by parenthetical term.

Note: The Library of Congress is now filing a parenthetical subject before an inverted subject in all cases, even though this order brings together unconnected subjects, e.g., MASS (CANON LAW) and MASS (CHEMISTRY) and introduces an unrelated subject between a simple subject and the same subject with an inversion. An exception is made for the names of literatures followed by the parenthetical terms (COLLECTIONS) and (SELECTIONS, EXTRACTS, ETC.), which subjects are filed before group 2 above.

    (7) Inverted subject headings. Arrange alphabetically by word following comma.

        An inverted place name, e.g., AFRICA, NORTH, is to be regarded as a *different* subject and is to be arranged after all the groups of the general subject.

    (8) Phrase subject headings. Interfile alphabetically with titles and other headings beginning with the same word.

b) Arrange the further subdivisions of a subhead according to the above order.

```
ART
ART - BIBLIOGRAPHY
    - CATALOGS
    - HISTORY
    - HISTORY - 19TH CENTURY
    - HISTORY - 20TH CENTURY
    - PERIODICALS
ART - BERLIN
    - GREECE
    - HUNGARY
    - NEW YORK (CITY)
    - U.S.
ART, AMERICAN
     ANCIENT
     BAROQUE
     GREEK
     MEDIEVAL
     MUNICIPAL
     ORIENTAL
Art, v.1-      [title of a periodical]
Art, a commodity
ART AND MORALS
ART AND STATE
Art foliage
ART INDUSTRIES AND TRADE


ENGLISH LITERATURE
ENGLISH LITERATURE - BIBLIOGRAPHY
                   - TRANSLATIONS
                   - TRANSLATIONS FROM FRENCH
                   - TRANSLATIONS FROM GERMAN
                   - TRANSLATIONS INTO FRENCH
ENGLISH LITERATURE - OLD ENGLISH, see ANGLO-SAXON
                          LITERATURE
                   - MIDDLE ENGLISH (1100-1500)
                   - EARLY MODERN (TO 1700)
                   - 18TH CENTURY
                   - 19TH CENTURY
```

```
ENGLISH LITERATURE — CATHOLIC AUTHORS
                   — IRISH AUTHORS
                   — SCOTTISH AUTHORS
ENGLISH LITERATURE — AUSTRALIA, see AUSTRALIAN
                            LITERATURE
                   — CANADA, see CANADIAN LITERATURE
                   — LANCASHIRE
                   — YORKSHIRE


LIFE
LIFE — ORIGIN
LIFE (BIOLOGY)
LIFE, ELIXIR OF, see ELIXIR OF LIFE
LIFE, FUTURE, see FUTURE LIFE
LIFE, SPIRITUAL, see SPIRITUAL LIFE
The life beyond
LIFE-BOATS
Life on the ocean wave
LIFE-SAVING


COOKERY
COOKERY — BIBLIOGRAPHY
        — EARLY WORKS TO 1800
COOKERY (APPLES)
        (CEREALS)
        (OYSTERS)
COOKERY, AMERICAN
         MEXICAN
         MILITARY
         SPANISH
COOKERY FOR INSTITUTIONS
COOKERY FOR THE SICK


WAR
WAR — CASUALTIES (STATISTICS, ETC.)
WAR — ECONOMIC ASPECTS
WAR — RELIEF OF SICK AND WOUNDED
WAR (INTERNATIONAL LAW)
WAR, ARTICLES OF, see MILITARY LAW
WAR, DECLARATION OF
WAR, MARITIME (INTERNATIONAL LAW)
WAR AND RELIGION
War of the worlds
WAR-SHIPS


AFRICA
        — DESCRIPTION AND TRAVEL
        — HISTORY
        — STATISTICS
AFRICA, NORTH
AFRICA, SOUTH
            — ANTIQUITIES
            — HISTORY
```

```
U.S. — HISTORY
U.S. — HISTORY — BIBLIOGRAPHY
               — DRAMA
               — SOURCES
U.S. — HISTORY — COLONIAL PERIOD
               — COLONIAL PERIOD — FICTION
               — COLONIAL PERIOD — KING WILLIAM'S WAR,
                    1689-1697
               — COLONIAL PERIOD — QUEEN ANNE'S WAR,
                    1702-1713
               — COLONIAL PERIOD — FRENCH AND INDIAN WAR,
                    1755-1763
               — REVOLUTION
               — REVOLUTION — CAMPAIGNS AND BATTLES
               — REVOLUTION — CAUSES
               — REVOLUTION — REGIMENTAL HISTORIES
               — 1783-1865
               — CONFEDERATION,  1783-1789
               — CONSTITUTIONAL PERIOD,  1789-1809
               — WAR OF 1812
               — 1815-1861
U.S. — HISTORY, JUVENILE
             , LOCAL
             , MILITARY
             , NAVAL
```

35. Subject arrangement 2 (Simplified order)

a) Arrange a subject, its subheads, etc., in the following order: —

(1) Subject without subdivision.

(2) Form, subject and geographical subdivisions, inverted subject headings, and subject followed by a parenthetical term interfiled in one alphabet, disregarding punctuation.

Note: Libraries adopting this arrangement will find it desirable to adopt also a uniform method of punctuation in the headings, either a period or a dash. This is illustrated in the examples below.

(3) Period divisions, arranged chronologically.

ALTERNATIVE: Period divisions, except those under such subheads as HISTORY, POLITICS AND GOVERNMENT, FOREIGN RELATIONS, may be filed alphabetically in group 2 above, if preferred. See example under ENGLISH LITERATURE below.

(4) Phrase subject headings, interfiled with titles and other headings beginning with the same word.

```
ART
ART — AMERICAN
    — ANCIENT
    — BAROQUE
    — BERLIN
    — BIBLIOGRAPHY
```

```
            — DECORATIVE
            — EXHIBITIONS
            — FRANCE
            — GREEK
            — HISTORY
            — HISTORY.  19TH CENTURY
            — HISTORY.  20TH CENTURY
            — MEDIEVAL
            — MUNICIPAL
            — MUNICIPAL.  BOSTON
            — MUNICIPAL.  EXHIBITIONS
            — MUNICIPAL.  NEW YORK (CITY)
            — ORIENTAL
            — U.S.
    Art.  v.1-     [title of a periodical]
    Art, a commodity
    ART AND MORALS
    Art foliage
    ART INDUSTRIES AND TRADE

    COOKERY
    COOKERY — AMERICAN
            — APPLES
            — BIBLIOGRAPHY
            — CEREALS
            — HISTORY
            — MEXICAN
            — MILITARY
            — OYSTERS
            — SPANISH
    COOKERY FOR INSTITUTIONS

    ENGLISH LITERATURE
    ENGLISH LITERATURE — AUSTRALIA,  see  AUSTRALIAN
                                LITERATURE
                       — BIBLIOGRAPHY
                       — HISTORY AND CRITICISM
                       — IRISH AUTHORS
                       — LANCASHIRE
                       — PERIODICALS
                       — SCOTTISH AUTHORS
                       — YORKSHIRE
    ENGLISH LITERATURE — OLD ENGLISH,  see  ANGLO-SAXON
                                LITERATURE

                       — MIDDLE ENGLISH (1100-1500)
                       — EARLY MODERN (TO 1700)
                       — 19TH CENTURY
                       — 20TH CENTURY
```

ALTERNATIVE:

```
    ENGLISH LITERATURE — AUSTRALIA,  see  AUSTRALIAN
                                LITERATURE
                       — BIBLIOGRAPHY
```

```
                    – EARLY MODERN (TO 1700)
                    – IRISH AUTHORS
                    – LANCASHIRE
                    – MIDDLE ENGLISH (1100-1500)
                    – PERIODICALS
                    – 19TH CENTURY
                    – OLD ENGLISH,  see  ANGLO-SAXON
                            LITERATURE
                    – SCOTTISH AUTHORS
                    – 20TH CENTURY

LIFE
LIFE (BIOLOGY)
LIFE – ELIXIR OF,  see  ELIXIR OF LIFE
LIFE – FUTURE,  see  FUTURE LIFE
LIFE – ORIGIN
LIFE – SPIRITUAL,  see  SPIRITUAL LIFE
Life beyond
LIFE-BOATS
Life on the ocean wave
LIFE-SAVING

WAR
WAR – ARTICLES OF,  see  MILITARY LAW
      – CASUALTIES (STATISTICS  ETC.)
      – COST OF
      – DECLARATION OF
      – ECONOMIC ASPECTS
WAR (INTERNATIONAL LAW)
      – MARITIME (INTERNATIONAL LAW)
      – RELIEF OF SICK AND WOUNDED
WAR AND RELIGION
War of the worlds
WAR-SHIPS

U.S. HISTORY
U.S. HISTORY – BIBLIOGRAPHY
              – DRAMA
              – JUVENILE
              – LOCAL
              – MAPS,  see  U.S. – HISTORICAL GEOGRAPHY –
                      MAPS
              – MILITARY
              – NAVAL
              – PERIODICALS
              – COLONIAL PERIOD
              – REVOLUTION
              – 1815-1861
```

Note: Small libraries may prefer to adopt a single-alphabet arrangement by interfiling the subdivisions of a subject with the titles and other entries beginning with the same word, disregarding punctuation. *See* ART in the Comprehensive example, Appendix V.

36. References

File *See also* references after entries of the same heading but before further subdivision of the same.

```
CHILDREN
CHILDREN,  see also
CHILDREN — BIOGRAPHY
CHILDREN — CARE AND TREATMENT
CHILDREN — CARE AND TREATMENT,  see also
CHILDREN — CARE AND TREATMENT — BIBLIOGRAPHY
```

This order allows the user of the catalog to find what material the library has on a subject before being referred away from it. Some libraries prefer to file a *See also* reference *before* the entries for the same subject on the ground that the user of the catalog will thus be directed to the more specific subject that he may actually want without having to look through all of the general subject first.

37. Title arrangement

See also Basic rule (Rule 1); Initial article (Rule 7); Punctuation (Rule 8); Words spelled differently (Rule 10); Hyphened and compound words (Rule 11); Order of entries (Rule 24)

a) Arrange title headings that are the same alphabetically by the main entry, an anonymous title preceding the same title with an author.

b) Arrange different editions of the same title entry according to the rule adopted for arrangement under author (Rule 25: *a* 6).

```
The pioneers
Cooper, J.F.
    The pioneers.  Philadelphia, Carey & Lea, 1832
    ———— London, J.M. Dent, [1929]
    ———— London & N.Y., Macmillan, 1901
    ———— N.Y., J.H. Sears, [1925]
    The pioneers
Mackay, C.D.
    The play of the pioneers
    The pioneers
Oppenheim, James
    The pioneers
```

c) Arrange periodical and newspaper titles by the main part of the title, disregarding the explanatory subtitle following a semicolon or comma since this not familiarly known as part of the title.

```
ASIA
Asia; journal of the American        Motor; the national
      Asiatic association                    monthly
Asia, an economic and regional       Motor age
      geography                       Motor world
Asia and Europe
```

d) Periodicals of the same title are arranged first by the place of publication and then by the date. The subtitle may be regarded if needed to distinguish between titles.

```
International review, an illustrated monthly journal.
                          La Crosse, Michigan
International review.  London, 1889
International review.  London, 1913-
International review.  N.Y.
International review.  Zurich
```

e) A periodical title used as an author entry is arranged after the entry of the periodical itself.

```
Power  [a magazine]
Power
  The second Power kink book
Power  [title of a book by Lucke]
Review of reviews; monthly
Review of reviews
  150 years ago
Review of reviews
  Pittsburgh; a new great city
```

f) Inverted titles may be arranged in either of two ways. *The alternative is recommended where the prevailing arrangement in the catalog is alphabetical.*

(1) File an inverted title before a longer running title beginning with the same word or phrase. Disregard an article preceding the inversion.

```
Personality, The family and
Personality, Integration of
Personality, Physical basis of
Personality culture
Personality plus
```

(2) ALTERNATIVE RULE: Interfile an inverted title alphabetically with other titles beginning with the same word, disregarding both the punctuation and an initial article preceding the inversion.

```
Personality culture
Personality, The family and
Personality in boys
Personality, Integration of
Personality, Physical basis of
Personality plus
```

Note: Inverted titles should seldom be made, because the catchword title alone (i.e., without the inverted part) or a corresponding subject entry or subject reference will usually meet all needs. The inverted part should be added only when the sense would be defec-

tive without it, or when the full title does not appear in the body
of the card. The inverted titles used in the above example to illustrate the arrangement are unnecessary if the subject heading PER-
SONALITY has been used.

38. Numerical and chronological arrangement

See also Numerals at beginning of title (Rule 9); Subject arrangement: period subheads (Rules 35:*a* 3 and 36:*a* 3)

A numerical or a chronological arrangement, rather than an alphabetical, should be made when number or date distinguishes between
entries, or headings, otherwise identical.

a) Numbered or dated series

```
      The American nation: a history.  v.2
Farrand, Livingston
      Basis of American history

      The American nation: a history.  v.3
Bourne, E. G.
      Spain in America

More, Paul Elmer
      Aristocracy and justice: Shelburne essays,  Ninth
         series
More, Paul Elmer
      Shelburne essays.  First series
More, Paul Elmer
      Shelburne essays.  Second series
More, Paul Elmer
      Shelburne essays.  Fourth series
More, Paul Elmer
      Shelburne essays.  Eighth series
More, Paul Elmer
...Shelburne essays.  Ninth series
         see his  Aristocracy and justice
More, Paul Elmer
...Shelburne essays.  Eleventh series
         see his  With the wits
More, Paul Elmer
      With the wits; Shelburne essays, Eleventh series

Atlantic readers. Primer
Atlantic readers. Bk. 1, grade IV
Atlantic readers. Bk. 3, grade VI
Atlantic readers. Bk. 4, grade VII
Atlantic readers. Bk. 6, grade VIII

      Bohlen lectures, 1891
Huntington, W. R.
      Peace of the church

      Bohlen lectures, 1899
Nash, H. S.
      Ethics and revelation
```

Bohlen lectures, 1925
Bell, W. C.
   Sharing in creation

b) Conferences, congresses, etc.

American peace congress. 1st, New York, 1907
American peace congress. 3rd, Baltimore, 1911
American peace congress. 4th, St. Louis, 1913

Massachusetts. Constitutional convention. 1779-1780
Massachusetts. Constitutional convention. 1856
Massachusetts. Constitutional convention. 1917-1919

c) Regiments, brigades, etc.

U.S. infantry. 2d regt., 1791-
U.S. infantry. 11th regt., 1861-
U.S. infantry. 21st regt., 1899-1902
U.S. infantry. 315th regt., 1917-1919
U.S. infantry. 332d regt., Co. D, 1917-1919

Georgia infantry. 3d brigade
Georgia infantry. 4th brigade
Georgia infantry. Anderson's brigade
Georgia infantry. Doles-Cook brigade
Georgia infantry. 2d regt.
Georgia infantry. 8th regt.

d) Laws, statutes, etc.

Gt. Brit. Laws, statutes, etc.
Gt. Brit. Laws, statutes, etc., 1066-1087 (William I)
Gt. Brit. Laws, statutes, etc., 1509-1547 (Henry VIII)
Gt. Brit. Laws, statutes, etc., 1625-1643 (Charles I)

e) Legislatures

U.S. Congress
U.S. CONGRESS
U.S. Congress. Committee on the census
         . Conference committees, 1897
         . Conference committees, 1908-1909
         . House
         . HOUSE
         . House. Committee on agriculture
         . House. Committee on foreign affairs
         . Joint commission of agricultural inquiry
         . Joint committee on Muscle Shoals
         . Select joint committee on the Harriman
                 geographic code system
         . Senate
         . Senate. Committee on appropriations
         . Senate. Committee on insular affairs
U.S. 1st Cong., 1789-1791. House
     2d Cong., 1st sess., 1791-1792
     41st Cong., 2d sess., 1869-1870

```
41st Cong., 3rd sess., 1870-1871
41st Cong., 3rd sess., 1870-1871.  House
62d Cong., 1st sess., 1911
62d Cong., 1st sess., 1911.  Senate
```

The above arrangement keeps an alphabetic order down to the point where the numbered Congresses begin and is recommended for that reason.

Appendix I

17:a. Forename entries. Arrangement 1 (Before surname)

Charles (<u>forename</u>)
    Charles, archduke of Austria, <u>see</u> Karl, <u>etc</u>.
    Charles, count of Angoulême, duke of Orléans, <u>see</u>
        Charles d'Orléans
    Charles, count of Valois
    Charles, le Téméraire, duke of Burgundy
    Charles II, duke of Lorraine
    Charles V, emperor of Germany
    Charles II, le Chauve, king of France
    Charles IV, le Bel, king of France
    Charles IX, king of France
    Charles, the Great, king of the Franks, <u>see</u>
        Charlemagne
    Charles I, king of Great Britain
    Charles, père
Charles (<u>compound</u>, <u>etc</u>., <u>forenames</u>)
    Charles Alexander, duke of Lorraine
    Charles Borromeo, Saint, <u>see</u> Carlo Borromeo, Saint
    Charles d'Orléans
    Charles de France, duke of Berry
    Charles Emanuel I, duke of Savoy, <u>see</u> Carlo
        Emanuele I, <u>etc</u>.
    Charles, le Téméraire, <u>see</u> Charles, duke of
        Burgundy (le Téméraire)
    Charles Louis de Bourbon, duke of Parma
    Charles Martel, mayor of the palace
    Charles, the Bald, <u>see</u> Charles II, king of France
        (le Chauve)
    Charles, the Bold, <u>see</u> Charles, duke of Burgundy
        (le Téméraire)
    Charles, the Great, <u>see</u> Charlemagne
Charles (<u>surname</u>)
    Charles, David
Charles (<u>titles</u>, <u>etc</u>.)
    Charles
    Charles Auchester, a novel
    Charles the Second, a play

Mary (forename)
  Mary,   princess of Great Britain
  Mary,   princess royal of England and princess of Orange
  Mary,   queen consort of George V
  Mary,   queen consort of James V, king of Scotland
  Mary,   queen consort of Louis XII, king of France
  Mary I, queen of England
  Mary II, queen of Great Britain
  Mary,   queen of Scots, see Mary Stuart, queen of
     the Scots
  Mary, Saint, of Egypt
  Mary, Virgin
Mary (compound, etc., forenames)
  Mary Adelaide Wilhelmina Elizabeth, duchess of Teck
  Mary Clare, sister
  Mary de Lellis, sister. see Gough, Sister Mary
     de Lellis
  Mary Magdalene, Saint
  Mary, of Bethany, Saint
  Mary, of Magdala, see Mary Magdalene, Saint
  Mary of Modena, queen consort of James II
  Mary of St. Angela, mother
  Mary of the Visitation, sister
  Mary Stuart, queen of the Scots
  Mary Victor, sister
Mary (surname)
  Mary, Albert
  Mary, Jules
Mary (titles, etc.)
  Mary and Anna
  Mary Celeste (brig)
  Mary of Scotland, a play
  Mary Stuart, a play

Thomas (forename)
  Thomas, archdeacon of Spalato, see Thomas Spalatensis,
     archdeacon
  Thomas, bp. of Marga
  Thomas, earl of Lancaster
  Thomas, Saint, apostle
Thomas (compound, etc., forenames)
  Thomas à Becket, Saint, abp. of Canterbury
  Thomas à Kempis
  Thomas, Anglo-Norman poet
  Thomas Aquinas, Saint
  Thomas Aquinas, sister
  Thomas Becket, Saint, see Thomas à Becket,
     Saint, etc.
  Thomas Brabantinus, see Thomas, de Cantimpré
  Thomas, de Burton
  Thomas, de Cantimpré
  Thomas Kempis, see Thomas à Kempis
  Thomas, of Capua, cardinal

Thomas, of Erceldoune, called the Rhymer
Thomas, of Kent
Thomas, the Rhymer, see Thomas, of Erceldoune,
    called the Rhymer
Thomas Spalatensis, archdeacon
Thomas, von Imbroich
Thomas (surname)
Thomas, Abram Owen
Thomas, Samuel Bell
Thomas (compound surname)
Thomas-Caraman, Charles
Thomas de Saint Laurent, Raymond de
Thomas-San-Galli, Wolfgang Alexander
Thomas (titles, etc.)
Thomas À Becket, a tragedy
Thomas à Kempis and Wales
Thomas of Reading [anonymous classic]
Thomas von Kandelberg [anonymous classic]

18. Forename entries. Arrangement 2 (After surname)

Mary (surname)
Mary, Albert
Mary, Jules
Mary-Lafon, Jean Bernard Lafon, called[1]
Mary (forenames, titles, etc.)
Mary [a title]
Mary Adelaide Wilhelmina Elizabeth, duchess of Teck
Mary and Anna
Mary Celeste (brig)
Mary Clare, sister
Mary de Lellis, sister, see Gough, Sister Mary
    de Lellis
Mary Feodorovna, empress consort of Paul I, emperor
    of Russia
Mary Magdalene, Saint
Mary, of Bethany, Saint
Mary of St. Angela, mother
Mary of Scotland, a play
Mary of the Visitation, sister
Mary, princess of Great Britain
Mary, princess royal of England and princess of Orange
Mary, queen consort of George V
Mary, queen consort of James V, king of Scotland
Mary, queen consort of Louis XII, king of France
Mary I, queen of England
Mary II, queen of Great Britain
Mary, queen of Scots, see Mary Stuart, queen of
    the Scots
Mary Rose Gertrude, sister
Mary, Saint, of Egypt

[1] If Rule 20: b, is adopted, this compound surname will file with the forenames,
titles, etc.

Mary Stuart [a play]
Mary Stuart, queen of the Scots
Mary Tudor [a play]
Mary Tudor, queen of England, see Mary I, queen
    of England
Mary Tudor, queen of France, see Mary, queen consort
    of Louis XII, king of France
Mary Victor, sister
Mary, Virgin
Thomas (surname)
Thomas, Abram Owen
Thomas, Samuel Bell
Thomas (forenames, titles, etc.)
Thomas À Becket [a play]
Thomas à Becket, Saint, abp. of Canterbury
Thomas à Kempis
Thomas à Kempis and Wales
Thomas, Aquinas, Saint
Thomas, archdeacon of Spalato, see Thomas Spalatensis,
    archdeacon
Thomas Balch library
Thomas Becket, Saint, see Thomas à Becket, Saint,
    abp. of Canterbury
Thomas, bp. of Marga
Thomas Brabantinus, see Thomas, de Cantimpré
Thomas-Caraman, Charles[2]
Thomas Co., Georgia
Thomas, de Burton
Thomas, de Cantimpré
Thomas de Saint Laurent, Raymond[2]
Thomas, earl of Lancaster
Thomas Edessenus, see Thomas, of Edessa
Thomas family
Thomas iron company
Thomas Kempis, see Thomas à Kempis
Thomas Margensis, see Thomas, bp. of Marga
Thomas, of Capua, cardinal
Thomas, of Edessa
Thomas, of Erceldoune, called the Rhymer
Thomas, of Kent
Thomas of Reading [anonymous classic heading]
Thomas, of Spalato, archdeacon, see Thomas
    Spalatensis, archdeacon
Thomas, Saint, apostle
Thomas-San-Galli, Wolfgang Alexander[2]
Thomas Spalatensis, archdeacon
Thomas, the Rhymer, see Thomas, of Erceldoune, called
    the Rhymer
Thomas, von Imbroich
Thomas von Kandelberg [anonymous classic heading]

[2] If Rule 20: *a* is adopted, this compound surname will file after the single surnames and before the forenames, titles, etc.

31. Place arrangement (Grouped order)

a) Three-group order

New York

Note: New York is treated as an exception in most libraries and, whether the general arrangement is a three-group order (Rule 31:*a*) or a two-group order (Rule 31:*b*), the nonofficial public institutions are interfiled with societies, organizations, titles, etc., and not with the official divisions under New York (City), New York (State), etc. (Cf. Rule 31:*a* 1, *Note.*)

```
New York (City)   (Author)
                  Aqueduct commission
                  Board of water supply
                  Bureau of franchises
                  Charters
                  CHARTERS
                  Common council
                  Ordinances
                  Police dept.
                  POLICE DEPT
                  Public library
                      see  New York.  Public library in the
                           file of Institutions, etc.,
                           following.
                  Stock exchange
                      see  New York.  Stock exchange in the
                           file of Institutions, etc.,
                           following.
NEW YORK (CITY)   (Subject)
                  — BIOGRAPHY
                  — CHARITIES
                  — HISTORY
                  — POLICE
                  — WATER SUPPLY
New York (colony)
                  Governor
                  Laws, statutes, etc.
                  — COMMERCE
                  — HISTORY
New York (county) District attorney's office
                  Register
                  Surrogate's court
New York (state)  (Author)
                  Adirondack survey
                  Chamber of Commerce
                      see  New York.  Chamber of commerce of
                           the state of New York in the
                           file of Institutions, etc.,
                           following.
                  Constitution
                  CONSTITUTION
```

```
                    Dept of health
                    Forest commission
                    Governor
                    Industrial board
                    Judicial council
                    State library, Albany
                       see  New York.  State library in the
                               file of Institutions, etc.,
                               following.
                    Museum
                       see  New York state museum in the
                               file of Institutions, etc.,
                               following.
                    University
    NEW YORK (STATE) (Subject)
                    ANTIQUITIES
                    DESCRIPTION AND TRAVEL
                    HISTORY
    New York  (Institutions, titles, etc.)
    New York  [title of a poem]
    New York academy of medicine
    New York aquarium
    New York.  Bar of the city of New York
    New York.  Chamber of commerce of the state of New York
    New York.  Citizens
    New York.  City and country school
    New York city council of political reform
    New York collection of music
    New York.  College of the city of New York
    New York county lawyers association
    New York day by day
    New York historical society
    New York.  Public library
    New York society library
    New York.  State library, Albany
    New York state museum
    New York.  Stock exchange
    New York university
    NEW YORK UNIVERSITY
    NEW YORK UNIVERSITY.  HALL OF FAME
    New York.  University club


    United States  (Author)
                 ,  appellant
                 ,  complainant
                 ,  petitioner
                 ,  plaintiff
                 .  Agricultural adjustment administration
                 .  Agriculture, Dept. of,  see
                 .     U.S. Dept. of agriculture
                 .  Army
```

- ARMY see entries in Subject file
    following.[3]
- Army. A.E.F., 1917-1919
- Army Air corps
- Bureau of the census
- Cavalry, see U.S. cavalry in the file of
    Titles, organizations, etc., follow-
    ing.
- Cavalry school, Fort Riley, Kansas
- Census, Bureau of the, see
    U.S. Bureau of the census
- Census office, 6th, 1840
- Census office, 7th, 1850
- Congress (for arrangement under Congress
    see Rule 39:c)
- Constitution
- CONSTITUTION[4]
- Dept. of agriculture
- Forest experiment station, Southern,
    New Orleans
- Forest service
- Laws, statutes, etc.[5]
- Navy dept.
- Penitentiary, Atlanta, Ga.
- Sugar equalization board, see
    United States sugar equalization board
    in the file of Titles, organizations,
    etc. following
- Treaties (arr. by date in heading)
- War Dept.

UNITED STATES   (Subject)
- — AGRICULTURE, see AGRICULTURE — U.S.
- — ANTIQUITIES
- — ARMY
- — ARMY — CAVALRY
- — ARMY — HISTORY
- — ARMY — INFANTRY
- — BOUNDARIES
- — CLAIMS VS GREAT BRITAIN
- — CONSTITUTION, see entries in Author file
    preceding.
- — FOREIGN RELATIONS
- — FOREIGN RELATIONS (arr. by form
    divisions)
- — FOREIGN RELATIONS (arr. by period
    divisions)
- — FOREIGN RELATIONS (arr. by country
    divisions)

[3] Subject entries for U.S.-Army and U.S.-Navy are probably better in the *Subject* file but may be kept in the *Author* file, if preferred.
[4] Subject entries for U.S.-Constitution may be put in the *Subject* file, if preferred.
[5] When entries are numerous, subarrange by subject of the laws, which may be included in the heading or at the upper-right corner of the cards.

```
                    —  HISTORY  (for subarr. see example under
                          Rule 35)
                    —  NAVY
                    —  RELATIONS (GENERAL) WITH CHINA
                    —  RELATIONS (GENERAL) WITH FRANCE
         United States  (Institutions, titles, etc.)
            United States abridged life tables
            U.S. air service  [a periodical]
            United States album
            United States conference of mayors
            United States housing corporation
            United States-Mexican commission
            United States naval institute, Annapolis
            United States navy  [a title]
            U.S. official pictures of the war
            United States sanitary commission
            United States steel corporation
            United States sugar equalization board
            U.S. tax cases
```

32. Place arrangement (Alphabetic order)

```
         New York  [title of a poem]6
         New York academy of medicine
         New York.  Agricultural experiment station, Geneva
         New York almanacs
         New York aquarium
         New York association for the blind
         New York.  Bar of the city of New York
         New York.  Bar of the state of New York
         New York (battleship)
         New York.  Bellevue hospital
         New York.  Board of trade and transportation
         New York botanical garden
         New York cavalry.  10th regt.
         New York.  Chamber of commerce of the state of New York
         New York.  Citizens
         New York (City)
         NEW YORK (CITY)
         NEW YORK (CITY) — AMUSEMENTS
         NEW YORK.  CITY AND COUNTRY SCHOOL
         NEW YORK (CITY) — BIOGRAPHY
         New York (City)  Board of education
         New York city boys
         NEW YORK (CITY) — CHARITIES
         New York (City)  Charters
         New York (City)  Common council
         New York city council of political reform
         NEW YORK (CITY) — WATER SUPPLY
         New York.  Civic repertory theatre
         New York collection of music
         New York.  College of physicians and surgeons
```

---

6 Cf. Rule 24: b 4.

New York.   College of the city of New York
New York.   Collegiate church
New York (Colony)
NEW YORK (COLONY) — COMMERCE
New York (Colony) <u>Governor</u>
New York (Colony) <u>Laws</u>, <u>statutes</u>, <u>etc</u>.
New York.   Cotton exchange
New York (County)   Court house
New York county lawyers association
New York (County)   <u>Surrogate's</u> <u>court</u>
New York day by day
New York historical society
New York.   Public library
New York school of social work
New York.   Sing Sing prison, Ossining
New York society library
New York (State)
New York (State)   Adirondack survey
NEW YORK (STATE) — ANTIQUITIES
New York (State)   Constitution
NEW YORK (STATE)   CONSTITUTION
New York (State)   Dept. of health
NEW YORK (STATE) — HISTORY
NEW YORK (STATE) — HISTORY — COLONIAL PERIOD
NEW YORK (STATE) — HISTORY — REVOLUTION
NEW YORK (STATE) — HISTORY — CIVIL WAR
New York (State)   Judicial council
New York.   State library, Albany
New York.   State library school, Albany
New York state library school association, inc.
New York state museum
New York (State)   University
New York.   Stock exchange
New York Times
New York.   Union theological seminary
New York university
New York.   University club
New York university. Hall of fame

United States
United States, appellant
United States, complainant
United States, plaintiff
UNITED STATES
United States abridged life table
U.S.   Agricultural adjustment administration
U.S. — AGRICULTURE, <u>see</u> AGRICULTURE — U.S.
U.S.   Agriculture, Dept. of, <u>see</u> U.S. Dept. of
    agriculture
U.S. air service [a periodical]
United States album
U.S. — ANTIQUITIES
U.S.   Army

U.S. — ARMY
U.S.   Army. A.E.F., 1917-1919
U.S.   Army. Air corp
U.S. — ARMY — CAVALRY
U.S.   ARMY — HISTORY
U.S. — BOUNDARIES
U.S.   Bureau of the census
U.S.   CAVALRY, _see_ U.S. ARMY. CAVALRY
U.S.   cavalry. 5th regt., 1855-
U.S.   Cavalry school, Fort Riley, Kan.
U.S. — CENSUS
U.S.   Census, Bureau of. _see_ U.S. Bureau of the census
U.S.   Census office, 6th, 1840
U.S.   Census office, 7th, 1850
U.S. — CLAIMS VS GREAT BRITAIN
U.S. — CLAIMS VS MEXICO
United States conference of mayors
U.S.   Congress (for arr. of subdivision _see_ example under
          Rule 39:c)
U.S.   Constitution
U.S.   CONSTITUTION
U.S.   CONSTITUTION — BIBLIOGRAPHY
U.S.   Constitution. 18th amendment
U.S.   Dept. of agriculture
U.S.   DEPT. OF AGRICULTURE
U.S.   Dept. of agriculture. Forest service, _see_ U.S.
          Forest service
U.S. — ECONOMIC CONDITIONS
U.S. — FOREIGN RELATIONS
U.S. — FOREIGN RELATIONS [form and country divisions
          interfiled]
U.S. — FOREIGN RELATIONS [period divisions arr.
          chronologically]
U.S.   Forest experiment station, Southern, New Orleans
U.S.   Forest service
U.S.   Geological survey
U.S. — HISTORY (for arr. of subdivision _see_ example
          under Rule 36)
United States housing corporation
U.S.   infantry. 63rd regt., 1917-1919
U.S.   Laws, statutes, etc.
United States. Medical research laboratory, Mineola, L.I.
United States merchant marine
United States-Mexican commission
United States-Mexico trade conference, 1st, Mexico (City),
          1920
United States naval institute, Annapolis
U.S.   NAVY
United States navy [a title]
U.S.   Navy dept.
U.S.   official pictures of the world war
U.S.   Penitentiary, Atlanta, Ga.
U.S. — RELATIONS (GENERAL) WITH CHINA

U.S. — RELATIONS (GENERAL) WITH FRANCE
United States sanitary commission
United States steel corporation
U.S. tax cases
U.S. War dept.

Appendix II

INITIAL ARTICLES TO BE DISREGARDED IN FILING

Dutch	French	German	Hun-garian	Italian	Nor-wegian	Portu-guese	Ruman-ian	Spanish
de	l'	*der (m.	a	il, lo	den, den	o	l, le	el, los
het	le	nom.)	az	i, gl', gli	det, den	a		la, las
't	la	die	egy	la, le	de, dei	os	un, o	
	les	das		l'		as		un, uno
een					en, ein			una, unas
eene	un	ein		un, uno	et { ei, e	um		
	une	eine		una, un	{ eit	uma		

* *der* as gen. pl. is to be regarded.

Appendix III

TABLE OF NUMERALS

	Danish	Dutch	French	German	Italian	Latin
1	en (een)	een	un, une	ein	uno	unus, una, unum
2	to	twee	deux	zwei	duo	duo, duae, duo
3	tre	drie	trois	drei	tre	tre, tria
4	fire	vier	quatre	vier	quattro	quattuor
5	fem	vijf	cinq —	fünf	cinque	quinque
6	seks	zes	six	sechs	sei	sex
7	syv	zeven	sept	sieben	sette	septem
8	otte	acht	huit	acht	otto	octo
9	ni	negen	neuf	neun	nove	novem
10	ti	tien	dix	zehn	dieci	decem
11	elleve	elf	onze	elf	undici	undecim
12	tolv	twaalf	douze	zwölf	dodici	duodecim
13	tretten	dertien	treize	dreizehn	tredici	tredecim
14	fjorten	veertien	quatorze	vierzehn	quattordici	quattuordecim
15	femten	vijftien	quinze —	fünfzehn	quindici	quindecim
16	seksten	zestien	seize	sechzehn	sedici	sedecim
17	sytten	zeventien	dix-sept	siebzehn	diciasette	septemdecim
18	atten	achtien	dix-huit	achtzehn	diciotto	duodeviginta
19	nitten	negentien	dix-neuf	neunzehn	dicianovo	undeviginta
20	tyve	twintig	vingt	zwanzig	venti	viginti
21	en og tyve	een en twintig	vingt et un	ein und zwanzig	ventuno	viginti unus
30	tredive	dertig	trente	driessig	trenta	triginta
40	fyrretyve	veertig	quarante	vierzig	quaranta	quadraginta
50	halvtred-sindstyve	vijftig	cinquante	fünfzig	cinquanta	quinquaginta
60	tresindstyve	zestig	sioxante	sechzig	sessanta	sexaginta
70	halvfjerd-sindstyve	zeventig	soixante-dix	siebzig	settanta	septuaginta
80	firsindstyve	tachtig	quatre-vingt	achtzig	ottanta	octoginta
90	halvfem-sindstyve	negentig	quatre-vingt-dix	neunzig	novanta	nonaginta
100	hundrede	honderd	cent	hundert	cento	centum
1000	tusinde	duizend	mille (mil)*	tausend	mille	mille
million		miljoen	million	million	milione	decies centena millia

* *Mil* is used in dates.

TABLE OF NUMERALS

	Norwegian*		Portuguese	Spanish	Swedish
1	ein, ei, eit	(en, ett)	um, uma	un, uno, una	en, ett, ene (a)
2	tvo	(to)	dois, dous, duas	dos	tvá
3	tri	(tre)	tres	tres	tre
4	fire		quatro	cuarto	fyra
5	fem		cinco	cinco	fem
6	seks		seis	seis	sex
7	sju	(syv)	sete	siete	sju
8	åtte	(otte)	oito	ocho	åtta
9	ni		nove	nueve	nio
10	ti		dez	diez	tio
11	elleve		onze	once	elva
12	tolv		doze	doce	tolv
13	trettan	(tretten)	treze	trece	tretton
14	fjortan	(fjorten)	quatorze	catorce	fjorton
15	femtan	(femten)	quinze	quince	femton
16	sekstan	(seksten)	dezeseis	diez y seis	sexton
17	syttan	(sytten)	dezesete	diez y siete	sjutton
18	attan	(atten)	dezoito	diez y ocho	aderton
19	nittan	(nitten)	dezenove	diez y nueve	nitton
20	tjuge	(tyve)	vinte	veinte	tjugu (tjugo)
21	ein og tjuge	(en og tyve)	vinte e um	veintiuno (veinte y uno)	tjuguen (tjuguett)
30	tretti	(tredve)	trinta	treinta	trettio
40	fyrti	(firti)	quarenta	cuarenta	fyrtio
50	femti		cincoenta	cincuenta	femtio
60	seksti		sessenta	sesenta	sextio
70	sytti		setenta	setenta	sjuttio
80	åtti	(otti)	oitenta	ochenta	attio
90	nitti		noventa	noventa	nittio
100	hundrad	(hunrede)	cem	cien, ciento	hundra
1000	tusund	(tusen)	mil	mil	tusen
million			milhão	millon	

* The numerals on the left belong to the "Landsmal;" those in curves are the variations of the "Riksmal."

Appendix IV

CANONICAL ARRANGEMENT

The order is that of the English authorized version with insertion of the names of groups of books before the first book in the group

52. Zephaniah
53. Haggai
54. Zechariah
55. Malachi
56. Apocrypha and Apocryphal books
57. Apocrypha
58. Apocrypha. Baruch
59. Apocrypha. Bel and the Dragon
60. Apocrypha. Ecclesiasticus
61. Apocrypha. Esdras
62. Apocrypha. 1 Esdras
63. Apocrypha. 2 Esdras
64. Apocrypha. History of Susanna
65. Apocrypha. Judith
66. Apocrypha. Maccabees
67. Apocrypha. 1 Maccabees
68. Apocrypha. 2 Maccabees

69. Apocrypha. Prayer of Manasses
70. Apocrypha. Rest of Esther
71. Apocrypha. Song of the Three Holy Children
72. Apocrypha. Tobit
73. Apocrypha. Wisdom of Solomon
74. Apocryphal books
75. Apocryphal books, A-Z [Individual apocryphal books in alphabetical order]
76. New Testament
77. Gospels and Acts
78. Gospels
79. Matthew
80. Mark

81. Luke and Acts
82. Luke
83. Johannine literature
84. John
85. Acts, Epistles and Revelation
86. Acts and Epistles
87. Acts
88. Epistles and Gospels, Liturgical
89. Epistles and Revelation
90. Epistles
91. Epistles of Paul
92. Romans
93. Corinthians
94. 1 Corinthians
95. 2 Corinthians
96. Galatians
97. Ephesians
98. Philippians
99. Colossians
100. Thessalonians
101. 1 Thessalonians

102. 2 Thessalonians
103. Pastoral epistles
104. Timothy
105. 1 Timothy
106. 2 Timothy
107. Titus
108. Philemon
109. Hebrews
110. Catholic epistles
111. James
112. Peter
113. 1 Peter
114. 2 Peter
115. Epistles of John
116. 1 John
117. 2 John
118. 3 John
119. Jude
120. Revelation
121. Apocryphal books
122. Apocryphal books, A-Z [Individual apocryphal books in alphabetical order]

Appendix V

29   Bible (Alphabetic order) *See Note* following the example for a still more simple arrangement.
32   Place arrangement (Alphabetic order)
35   Subject arrangement (Alphabetic order) *See Note* following example for a still more simple arrangement.
36   *See also* references
37   Title arrangement *a, b, c, d, e, f2*
39   Chronological and numerical arrangements

The entries in the following comprehensive example are arranged according to the simplest alphabetical order, except that personal surnames precede other entries beginning with the same word (*see* Rule 24: *b*2). Small libraries may prefer to interfile personal names also.

COMPREHENSIVE EXAMPLE

```
A B C book
A. E.  see  Russell, George William
A., F. P.  see  Adams, Franklin Pierce
A.L.A.  see  American library association
A.L.A. booklist
À la mer
Aagard, Carl Johann
Abbot, Willis John
Abbott, Albert
Abbott, Miss E. C.
Abbott, Edith
'Abd  al-Hamīd II,  sultan of the Turks
'Abd al-Latīf
'Abd Allāh ibn Ahmad, called Ibn al-Baitar
'Abd Allāh Sfer,  pasha
'Abd el-Halim Kararah, Muhammad
Abdullah, Achmed
À Beckett, Arthur William
Abee, Fritz
About face
Abū al-'Alā
Abū al-Fidā
Abū Bakr ibn al-Tufail, Abu Ja'far
Abū Sa'īd
Abucacim
Abū'l 'Alā,  see  Abu al-'Alā
Abūl-Fazl,  mirza
L'abuse en court
R. Accademia dei Lincei, Rome
ACCIDENTS
1813; ein historischer roman  [achtzehnhundert zwölf]
American library association
American library association,  see also titles beginning
     A. L. A.
American peace congress,  1st, New York, 1907
American peace congress,  3rd, Baltimore, 1911
```

— — and ships and sealing wax
Andersen, Hans Christian
Anderson, Arthur
Anderson, James
Anderson's college, Glasgow
Anderssen, Adolf
Art, v.1 - [<u>title</u> <u>of</u> <u>a</u> <u>periodical</u>]
ART
  Brown, G.B. The fine arts
ART
  Brownell, Baker. Art in action
ART
  Thurston, C.H.P. Structure of art
Art: a commodity
Art age
ART — American
ART — Ancient
Art and Mrs Bottle
ART AND MORALS
ART — BERLIN
ART — BIBLIOGRAPHY
ART — DECORATIVE
Art foliage
ART — FRANCE
ART — GREEK
ART — HISTORY
ART INDUSTRIES AND TRADE
ART — MUNICIPAL
L'art romantique
ART — U.S.
Art weaving
Atlantic readers. Primer
Atlantic readers. Bk.1
Atlantic readers. Bk.3
Bible
  The Bible and its story
Bible
  Die Heiligen Schriften
Bible
  The Holy Bible... 1885
Bible
  The Holy Bible... 1904
Bible
  La Sainte Bible
Bible
  The Scofield reference Bible
BIBLE
BIBLE AND SCIENCE
BIBLE — ANTIQUITIES
Bible as literature
Bible beautiful
BIBLE — BIBLIOGRAPHY
A bible for freshmen

Bible music
Bible. N.T.
Bible. N.T.   Gospels
Bible. O.T.
BIBLE. O.T.
Bible. O.T.   Amos
Bible. O.T.   I Chronicles
Bible. O.T.   II Chronicles
Bible. O.T.   Daniel
BIBLE. O.T.   DANIEL
BIBLE. O.T. — HISTORY
Bible. O.T.   Pentateuch
Bible. Paraphrases
Bible plays [a title]
Bible. Selections
BIBLE — VERSIONS
Bibliothèque d'anthologie
Bibliothèque d'histoire
Bibliothèque de la révolution
Bohlen lectures, 1899
   Nash, H.S. Ethics and revelation
Bohlen lectures, 1925
   Bell, W.C. Sharing in creation
Böök, Fredrik
Book, William Frederick
The book about aircraft
BOOK-BINDING, see BOOKBINDING
BOOK COVERS
A book of garden flowers
BOOKBINDING
BOOKBINDING, see also BOOK COVERS
Bookbinding and the care of books
BOOKBINDING — EXHIBITIONS
BOOKBINDING — GREAT BRITAIN
BOOKBINDING — HISTORY
Bookbinding leather committee
BOOKBINDING — MOHAMMEDAN
BOOKBINDING — U.S.
The Bookman. London [a periodical]
The Bookman; a review of books and life. New York
The Bookman; an illustrated literary journal. New York
The Bookman
   Robert Louis Stevenson
The Bookman anthology of essays
The bookman's manual. 1935
The bookman's manual. 1928
BOOKS
Books; a weekly review
Books about books
Boy Scouts
BOYCOTT
BOYS' CLUBS
Boy's King Arthur

Boys of '76
Brown, Capt
Brown, Mrs
Brown, A. G.
Brown, Albert
Brown, John
Brown, John, pseud.
Brown, Sir John
Brown, John, 1716-1766
Brown, John, d.1811
Brown, John, 1810-1882
Brown America
Brown & Sharpe manufacturing co.
Brown brothers and company
Brown county almanack
BROWN CO., OHIO
BROWN CO., WISC.
BROWN FAMILY
Brown university
Brownbill, John
Browne, pseud.
Browne, A. K.
Caterina, <u>see also</u> Catherine
Caterina Cornaro, queen of Cyprus
Caterina da Siena, Saint
Caterina, Saint, of Bologna
Catesby, Mark
Catharina, <u>see</u> Catherine
Catharine, <u>see</u> Catherine
Cather, Willa Sibert
Catherine, <u>see also</u> Caterina; Katherine
Catherine [<u>a title</u>]
Catherine de Gardeville [<u>a title</u>]
Catherine de Médicis, queen consort of Henry II,
    king of France
Catharine I, empress of Russia
Catharine Frances, sister
Catherine Howard [<u>a play</u>]
Catharine Howard, queen consort of Henry VIII
Catharine of Aragon, queen consort of Henry VIII
Catharine, of Bologna, Saint, <u>see</u> Caterina, Saint,
    of Bologna
Catharine of Braganza, queen consort of Charles II
Catharine of Siena, Saint, <u>see</u> Caterina da Siena,
    Saint
Catherine Parr, queen consort of Henry VIII
Catharine, Saint, of Bologna, <u>see</u> Caterina, Saint,
    of Bologna
Catharine, Saint, of Siena, <u>see</u> Caterina da Siena,
    Saint
Catherwood, Benjamin Franklin
Catholic church
CATHOLIC CHURCH

CATHOLIC CHURCH — BIOGRAPHY
Catholic church. Councils
CATHOLIC CHURCH — HISTORY
Catholic church. Pope
Charlemagne
Charles, David
Charles, William
Charles [a title]
Charles Alexander, duke of Lorraine
Charles Auchester, a novel
Charles Borromeo, Saint, see Carlo Borromeo, Saint
Charles City, Iowa
Charles d'Orléans
Charles Dickens in London
Charles, duke of Burgundy (le Téméraire)
Charles II, duke of Lorraine
Charles V, emperor of Germany, see Karl V, emperor of
     Germany
CHARLES FAMILY
Charles II, king of France
Charles IX, king of France
Charles I, king of Great Britain
Charles II, king of Great Britain
Charles Martel, mayor of the palace
The Charles men
Charles-Roux, François
Charles, the Bold, see Charles, duke of Burgundy
     (le Téméraire)
Charles, the Great, see Charlemagne
Charleston, S.C.
CHILDREN
CHILDREN, see also CHILD STUDY; YOUTH
CHILDREN — BIBLIOGRAPHY
CHILDREN — BIOGRAPHY
CHILDREN — CARE AND HYGIENE
CHILDREN — CARE AND HYGIENE; see also CHILDREN — NUTRI-
     TION; SCHOOL HYGIENE
Cicero, Marcus Tullius (Works by)
  Ars oratorio; selections
  Cato major de senectute
  Cicero's correspondence
  A defense of old age
  Letters to his friends
  Orations...ed. by Moore
  Orations...ed. by Yonge
  (Cicero): ten orations and selected letters
  The works of Cicero
CICERO, MARCUS TULLIUS (Works about)
  Boissier
    Cicero and his friends
  Conway
    Makers of Europe
      Caesar the destroyer. The originality of Cicero.

CICERO — BIBLIOGRAPHY
Concord, a poem
Concord and Lexington
Concord antiquarian society
CONCORD, BATTLE OF
Concord days
CONCORD, MAINE
Concord, Mass.
CONCORD, MASS.
Concord, Mass. Convention, July 14, 1774
CONCORD, MASS. — HISTORY
Concord, Mass. Trinity church
Concord, N.H.
Concord, N.H. Public library
Concord railroad corporation
CONCORD RIVER
CONCORD SCHOOL OF PHILOSOPHY
Concord, Tenn. Farragut school
Cooperative marketing
Co-operative movement
De la terre á la lune
De libris
Defoe, Daniel
De la Roche, Mazo
Delarue, A. O.
De La Rue, Warren
Delarue-Mardrus, Lucie
Delaware
Del Mar, Alexander
Dem dichter in der fernen bild geblieben [initial article
     not in nominative case]
DeMorgan, Joseph
Eine von zu vielen [numeral]
El Dorado
Eldorado, Neb.
El Paso, Texas
Eine kleine gefälligkeit [initial article]
Labour and industry
Labor economics
Laboulaye
Labour, see spelling Labor
Lang, Andrew
   Adventures among books

   Lang, Andrew, ed.
Lang, Mrs Leonora Blanche
   Book of saints and heroes

Lang, Andrew
   Homer and the epic

   Lang, Andrew, tr.
Homerus
   Iliad

Lang, Andrew
  The Maid of France
    The library has also this title in
    French: La Pucelle de France
Lang, Andrew
  The making of religion
  LANG, ANDREW
    THE MAKING OF RELIGION
Tyrrell, George
  The faith of the millions. v.2
Lang, Andrew
  La Pucelle de France
Lang, Andrew, ed.
  The red fairy book... il. by Ford and Speed
  _____ ... il. by Lee
  _____ ... il. by Tenggren

  Lang, Andrew, jt. auth.
Haggard, Sir H.H.
  The world's desire
  LANG, ANDREW
Gordon, G.S.
  Andrew Lang

Mach, Edmund
McHale, Kathryn
Machard, Alfred
McHardy, D.N.
Machen, Arthur
Machine design
MACHINERY
McHugh, John
MacLaren, J.M.
M'Laren, J.T.
McLaren, L.L.
MacLaren, R.S.
Mistress and maid
Mrs Dane's defense
Mistress of Husaby
Modern American writers, I
  Van Doren, C.C. James Branch Cabell
Modern American writers, II
  Lovett, R.M. Edith Wharton
Modern American writers, V
  Clark, B.H. Eugene O'Neill
Modern drama series
  Andreev, L.N. Savva
Modern drama series
  Becque, Henri. The vultures
Mrs.
  Entries beginning with Mrs. are filed as if spelled
  Mistress
Muel, Leon

Muellenbach, Ernst
Mueller
   See also Muller (or Müller)
Mueller, Alfred Don
Muenscher, Joseph
La muerta de Néron
Mugdan, Martin
MUKDEN, BATTLE OF, 1905
Mulcahy, William Francis
Muller (or Müller)
   See also Mueller
Müller, Adam
Muller, Adam L.
Müller, Carl Otto
Müller, Max
Münchener bienen-zeitung
New Amsterdam
NEW ENGLAND
New York academy of medicine
New York. Agricultural experiment station, Geneva
New York almanacs
New York (battleship)
New York cavalry. 10th regt.
New York (City)
New York (City) Board of education
NEW YORK (CITY) — CHARITIES
New York (City) Common council
New York city council of political reform
NEW YORK (CITY) — WATER SUPPLY
New York collection of music
New York. College of the city of New York
New York (Colony)
New York. Cotton exchange
New York (County) Court house
New York day by day
New York. Public library
New York school of social work
New York. Sing Sing prison, Ossining
New York (State)
NEW YORK (STATE)
New York (State) Dept of health
NEW YORK (STATE) — HISTORY
New York. State library, Albany
New York state museum
New York (State) University
New York Times
New York university
Newark, N.J.
Newman, John Henry, card.
De night in de front from Chreesmas [initial article]
1940 book of houses [nineteen forty]
1917 war tax guide [nineteen seventeen]
One hundred and one famous poems

```
100 bungalows
150 radio hook-ups  [one hundred fifty]
101 metal-working projects  [one hundred one]
PERSONALITY
Personality, The family and
Personality in boys
Personality, Integration of
Personality plus

   The pioneers
Cooper, J.F.
   The pioneers.  Philadelphia, Carey & Lea

   _____  London, J.M.Dent

   _____  New York, Sears

   The pioneers
Mackay, C.D.
   The play of the pioneers

   The pioneers
Oppenheim, James
   The pioneers

Saint M*****, Victor de,  see  Saint-Mauris,  Victor
     Alexandre,  comte de
Saint Malo, France
Saint Mark's school, Southborough, Mass.
St Mars, F.
Saint-Mars, Gabrielle Anne (Cisterne de Courteras)
     vicomtesse de
St Nicholas
St Paul, Henry
St Paul, Minn.
Saint Paul,  mother
Sainte Beuve, Charles Augustin
Saintine
San Francisco, Cal.
San José, Diego
San tzŭ ching
Sanborn, Albert J.
Santa Fé
Santa Marina, Luys
Santagnello, M.
Shakespeare  (Works by)
   A piacer vostro (As you like it)
   Aphorisms from Shakespeare
   As you like it   (Ben Greet Shakespeare)
   (Shakespeare's) As you like it, ed. by Cooper
   (The comedy of) As you like it  (Eclectic classics)
   As you like it  (New Temple Shakespeare)
   (Shakespeare's comedy of) As you like it, ed. by Rolfe
   As you like it
      The library has an Italian translation:
      A piacer vostro
   The beauties of Shakespeare
```

```
The college Shakespeare
Comedies, ed. by Craig
(Shakespeare's) Comedy of error
Complete works, ed. by Craig  (Oxford Shakespeare)
(Shakespeare's) dramatische werke
Edward III,  see  Edward III (Drama)
Julius Caesar, ed. by Mabie
(The plays of Shakespeare. The tragedy of) Julius
    Caesar, ed. by Sykes
King Richard III, a tragedy
Longman's school Shakespeare
(The comedy of) Much ado about nothing
Oxford Shakespeare; the complete works, ed. by Craig
Poetical works
Richard III,  see his  King Richard III
Songs and sonnets, ed. by Palgrave
Songs and sonnets, il. by Robinson
(Shakespeare's) sonnets
SONNETS
    Godwin.  A new study of the sonnets
    Hitchcock.  Remarks on the Sonnets
The taming of the shrew.  Coriolanus   Booklovers ed.
Taming of the shrew.  Garrick & Kemble
The taming of the shrew, a comic opera by Goetz  [a
    secondary entry with main entry under Goetz]
(Shakespeare's comedy of the) Taming of the shrew, ed.
    by Rolfe
TAMING OF THE SHREW
    Tolman.  Shakespeare's part in the "Taming of the
    shrew"
Two noble kinsmen,  see  Fletcher, John.  The two
    noble kinsmen
SHAKESPEARE   (Works about)
SHAKESPEARE — ADAPTATIONS
SHAKESPEARE — AUTHORSHIP
SHAKESPEARE — BIBLIOGRAPHY
SHAKESPEARE — CONCORDANCES, INDEXES, ETC.
10 story book
Tenberg, Rudolf
Ten Broeke, James
Un de Baumugnes  [numeral]
United States
United States abridged life tables
U.S.  Agricultural adjustment administration
U.S.  Agriculture, Dept of,  see  U.S.  Dept of
    agriculture
U.S. air service  [a periodical]
United States album
U.S. — ARMY
U.S. — ARMY — CAVALRY
U.S. — ARMY — HISTORY
U.S.  Bureau of the census
U.S. cavalry.  5th regt., 1855-
```

```
U.S.   Cavalry school, Fort Riley, Kan.
U.S. — CENSUS
U.S.   Census, Bureau of,  see  U.S.  Bureau of the census
U.S.   Census office. 7th census,  1850
U.S.   Census office. 11th census,  1890
U.S.   Congress
U.S.   CONGRESS
U.S.   Congress.  Committee on the census
U.S.   Congress.  House
U.S.   Congress.  House.  Committee on foreign affairs
U.S.   Congress.  Joint committee on Muscle Shoals
U.S.   Congress.  Office of legislative counsel
U.S.   Congress.  Senate
U.S.   Congress.  Senate.  Committee on appropriations
U.S.   Congress.  Senate.  Committee on insular affairs
U.S.   1st Cong., 1789-1791
U.S.   2d Cong., 1st sess., 1791-1792
U.S.   41st Cong., 2d sess., 1869-1870
U.S.   41st Cong., 3rd sess., 1870-1871
U.S.   Dept of agriculture
U.S.   DEPT OF AGRICULTURE
U.S.   Geological survey
U.S. — HISTORY
U.S. — HISTORY — BIBLIOGRAPHY
U.S. — HISTORY — DRAMA
U.S. — HISTORY — LOCAL
U.S. — HISTORY — NAVAL
U.S. — HISTORY — PERIODICALS
U.S. — HISTORY (BY PERIODS)
U.S. — HISTORY — COLONIAL PERIOD
                 — COLONIAL PERIOD — FICTION
                 — COLONIAL PERIOD — FRENCH AND INDIAN
                       WAR, 1755-1763
                 — REVOLUTION
                 — REVOLUTION — CAMPAIGNS AND BATTLES
                 — 1783-1865
                 — CONSTITUTIONAL PERIOD, 1789-1809
                 — WAR OF 1812
                 — 1815-1861
United States housing corporation
United States-Mexican commission
U.S. — NAVY
U.S.   Navy dept
U.S. official pictures of the world war
U.S.  Penitentiary, Atlanta, Ga.
United States steel corporation
WAR
WAR AND RELIGION
WAR,  ARTICLES OF,  see  MILITARY LAW
WAR — CASUALTIES (STATISTICS, ETC.)
WAR,  COST OF
WAR,  DECLARATION OF
WAR — ECONOMIC ASPECTS
```

```
WAR (INTERNATIONAL LAW)
WAR,  MARITIME (INTERNATIONAL LAW)
War of the worlds
WAR — RELIEF OF SICK AND WOUNDED
WAR-SHIPS
Washington, George
Washington academy of science
Washington Co., Ohio
Washington, D.C.
Washington, D.C.  WHITE HOUSE
Washington merry-go-round
Washington, Mt.
Washington (State)
WASHINGTON (STATE) — DESCRIPTION AND TRAVEL
Washington (State)  Geological survey
Washington (State)  State library, Olympia
Washington (Ter.)  Governor
Washington university, St. Louis
Who is who in America
Who'd be king
Whom the gods destroy
Who's who
Whose home is the wilderness
Ye that judge
```

Appendix VI

BIBLIOGRAPHY

*Separately Published Codes

Akers, S. G. *Simple library cataloging.* Chicago: American library association, 1933.
"Arrangement of cards in a catalog," p.132-44.

American library association. *Proceedings of the Catalog Section of the A.L.A.* Chicago: The Association, 1929.
"Committee on standardization of alphabeting practice, report, 1929, p.30-34."

*Barnstead, W. G. *Filing rules for dictionary catalogues.* 2d ed. Toronto: Ball, 1934. 14p.
Recommended by the Minister of education for use in the public libraries of Ontario.

Bishop, W. W. *Practical handbook of modern library cataloging.* Baltimore: Williams & Wilkins co., 1924.
"Filing." p.111-14.

British museum. Department of printed books. *Catalogue of printed books in the British museum.* Vol. 1. London: British museum, 1841.
"Rules for the compilation of the catalogue," p.v-ix.

Cambridge university. Library. *Rules for the catalogues of printed books, maps and music.* London: Macmillan, 1927.
"Arrangement in catalog," p.50-53.

Childs, J. B. "Rules for alphabetical filing by words in the dictionary catalog . . . together with 'Manchester,' a specimen of such filing." Urbana, Ill.: University of Illinois library school, 1921-22. Mimeographed.

*Cincinnati. Public library. *Filing rules for the arrangement of the dictionary catalog of the library; County library district of Hamil-

ton county, Ohio; comp. by A. E. Ewald and A. M. Dunlap. 3d ed. Cincinnati: Cincinnati public library, 1936. 64p.

Clapp, C. B. "Arrangement of cards under place names in a dictionary catalog," *Library Journal,* XXXVIII (February 1913), p.73-77.

*Cleveland. Public library. *Filing rules for the arrangement of the dictionary catalogs of the Cleveland public library.* Cleveland: Cleveland public library, 1922. 27p.

Cotts, C. W. "Fun (?) of filing." *Wilson Bulletin,* XXIX (March 1933), p.64-65.
Brief consideration of some differences of opinion in various alphabeting codes, which show the need of standardization of rules.

Cranshaw, J. "A word or two." *Library Assistant,* XXIX (November 1936), p.259-63.

Cunningham, A. D. "Dictionary catalogue." *New Zealand Library,* I (June 1938), p.85-87.
Arrangement of entries . . . with reference to analyticals, collections of works by or about a single author, geographical entries, etc.

Cutter, C. A. Rules for a dictionary catalog. 4th ed. Washington: Govt. print. off., 1904.
"Arrangement," p.111-21.

Dean, H. E. "Numerals vs. words." *Library Journal,* LVIII (June 15, 1933), p.559-60.
Details of a plan for writing out numerals in title, thus indicating the alphabetic arrangement.

*Dziatzko, K. F. O. *Instruction für die ordnung der titel im alphabetischen zettelkatalog der Königlichen und Universitäts-bibliothek zu Breslau.* Berlin. 1886. 74p.

Edmands, J. "Rules for alfabeting." *Library Journal,* XII (September, October 1887), p.326-31; p.431-35.

Hastings, C. H. "Proposed manual on the arrangement of cards in alphabetical catalogs." *Bulletin of the American Library Association,* IX (July 1915), 270-73.
Problems in alphabeting place names, subdivision under subjects, added entries, editions, books of the Bible and the umlaut listed.

Hitchler, T. *Cataloging for small libraries.* New York: Stechert, 1926. "Arrangement," p.262-69.

Holcomb, E. "Filing in the university of California." *Library Journal,* LX (March 15, 1935), p.257.

Description of a method which increases accuracy, lessens fatigue and cuts cost.

Illinois state library. Archives division. *Catalog rules; series for archives material.* Springfield, Ill.: Illinois state library, 1938.
"Guide cards and filing," p.4-6.

Jewett, C. C. *On the construction of catalogues of libraries, and their publication by means of separate stereotyped titles, with examples.* Washington: Smithsonian institution, 1853.
"Arrangement," p.59-69.

Kroeger, A. B. "Arrangement of entries in catalogs." *Public libraries,* X (January 1905), 18-19.
Mainly an analysis of differences between 3d and 4th editions of Cutter's rules for a dictionary catalog.

*Latshaw, R. N. "A comparative study of some rules for the alphabetical arrangement of entries in library catalogs." Urbana, Ill.: Univ. of Illinois, 1928. Typewritten.

Linderfelt, K. A. *Eclectic card catalog rules.* Boston: C. A. Cutter, 1890.
"Alphabetic arrangement of titles," p.46-75.

Mann, M. *Introduction to cataloging and the classification of books.* Chicago: American library association, 1930.
"Dictionary catalog—arrangement," p.221-29.

Mischoff, W. O. "Catalog from a reader's viewpoint." *Library Journal,* XLVII (December 15, 1932), p.1035-38.
Critical examination of methods of alphabeting.

Osborn, A. D. *Prussian instructions; rules in the alphabetical catalogs of the Prussian libraries.* Ann Arbor: Univ. of Michigan pr. 1938.

Arrangement of the like names of different authors, p.66-70; arrangement of like titles for different works, p.92; arrangement of the different editions and translations of the same work, p.92-104; alphabetical arrangement of authors' names and real titles, p.105-06.

Oxford university. Bodleian library. *Rules for the general catalogue of printed books.* Oxford, Oxford university pr. 1933.
"Alphabetization," Sect. 51-56.

*Pittsburgh. Carnegie library. *Rules for filing cards in the dictionary catalogues of the Carnegie library of Pittsburgh.* Pittsburgh: Carnegie library of Pittsburgh, 1932. 34p.

Preston, G. J. "Problems involved in an alphabetical arrangement of a library catalog." Urbana, Ill.: Univ. of Illinois, 1936. 143p. Typewritten.

I: Complex features of various filing codes; II: Filing rules for the arrangement of entries in a dictionary catalog; III: Problems involved in attempting a strictly alphabetical arrangement of a dictionary catalog; Conclusion: Bibliography.

(Abstracted in American library association. Catalog Section. *Catalogers' and classifiers' yearbook*. Number 6, 1937. Chicago: American library association, 1937. p.115-17.)

*Queens Borough public library. *Rules for filing cards in the catalogues of all departments and branches.* ₁Jamaica₁ Queens Borough public library, 1933. 47p.

Quinn, J. H., and H. W. Acomb. *Manual of cataloguing and indexing.* London: G. Allen & Unwin, ltd., 1933. "Alphabetical arrangement," p.249-54.

Ranganathan, S. R. *Classified catalogue code.* Madras: Madras library association, 1934. "Sequence of entries," p.35-42.

Rathbone, J. A., and F. R. Coe. "Simple filing rules." *Massachusetts Library Club Bulletin,* XXI (June 1931), 37-39.

Sharp, H. A. *Cataloguing.* London: Grafton, 1935. "Arrangement of catalogues," p.224-31.

Steele, H. G. "Note on alphabetic order." *Library World,* XV (February 1913), p.247-48. Includes a set of rules, p.248.

Stevens, Henry. *Catalogue of American books in the library of the British museum.* London: C. Whittingham, 1866. "Rules for the compilation of the Catalogue of printed books," p.ix-xxvii.

Thornton, J. L. *Cataloging in special libraries.* London: Grafton, 1938. 268p. "Filing in special libraries," p.239-45. Discussion of a number of disputed points.

Vatican. Biblioteca vaticana. *Norme per il catalogo degli stampati.* Città de Vaticano: Biblioteca, 1931. "Ordinamento delle schede nel catalogo alfabetico." p.341-71.

Wilson, M. *School library management.* N.Y.: Wilson, 1931. "Rules for arrangement of cards," by B. R. Barden, p.138-46.

Wilson, H. W. co. *Stylebook.* N.Y.: Wilson, 1921. 86p.
   "Alphabeting," p.13-19.

Wood, A. F. "California divides its catalog." *Library Journal,* LXIII
   (October 1, 1938), p.725-26.

   Detailed description of routine involved in changing catalog over
into an author and title and a subject section, consisting of "a division
within each tray of the authors and titles from the subjects."

Index

References in boldface type are to rule numbers; those preceded by p. indicate pages; Ex denotes reference to an example; references to footnotes are so marked.

This book, designed by Harold English, has been set in Textype and Remington Typewriter with underscore, both Linotype faces, printed on Opacitone Eggshell and bound in Interlaken Arco Linen Vellum. Cover design by Harold English and Joseph Trautwein. Composition by M & L Typesetting and Electrotyping Co.; presswork by Wisconsin Cuneo Press; binding by John F. Cuneo Co. The cover is water repellant and may be cleansed with a damp cloth.